EVERYTHING YOU
KNOW ABOUT MONEY IS
WRONG

EVERYTHING YOU
KNOW ABOUT MONEY IS

WRONG

OVERCOME THE FINANCIAL MYTHS
KEEPING YOU FROM THE LIFE YOU WANT

KAREN RAMSEY

ReganBooks
An Imprint of HarperCollinsPublishers

HarperCollins books may be purchased for educational, business, or sales promotional use. For information please write: Special Markets Department, HarperCollins Publishers, Inc., 10 East 53rd Street, New York, NY 10022.

FIRST EDITION

Designed by Joseph Rutt

Library of Congress Cataloging-in-Publication Data on file at the
Library of Congress
ISBN: 0-06-039273-8
97 98 99 00 01 ❖/RRD 10 9 8 7 6 5 4 3 2 1

This book is dedicated to:

—my parents
for laying the foundation from
which to launch myself;

—Jane Shearer
for her partnership,
without which none of this
would have been possible; and

—my clients
for continuing to be
my source of inspiration.

CONTENTS

INTRODUCTION

"Prosperity is living easily and happily in the real world, whether you have money or not."

—Jerry Gillies, author of
*Moneylove: How to Get Money
You Deserve for Whatever You
Want*

We're so screwed up about money. We think that it will solve all our troubles—that if we just had more money it would give us more freedom, more time, more peace, and more happiness in our lives. If we only had *more.*

For the past fifteen years I have provided personal financial counseling to hundreds of people who earn adequate income. Yet they come in to my office with the feeling that no matter what they do, they never have enough.

Perhaps you share this feeling. You work hard trying to provide for your family or to improve your lifestyle, and what you get in return is chronic burnout, perpetual stress, and a vague feeling that you will never get ahead. However, *there is nothing wrong with you and you are not alone.* Millions of people share this problem.

I wrote this book to reveal the faulty perceptions—the myths—that people like you have about money. These perceptions drive most of our lifestyle decisions—often in the wrong direction.

This isn't a book about how to become a millionaire or how to act like one when you aren't. It's not a book about the nuts and bolts of investing. It is a book about how much more prosperous you can become using only what you already have. It's about learning to live a more satisfied and contented life. It's about transforming your relationship with money so it can become a friendlier presence in your life.

This book offers practical advice for dealing with the day-to-day realities of money and how to overcome the frustrations that stem from financial problems. It is a guide for getting what you want *now*, while still providing for your future needs.

What if you could have more financial contentment in your life right now, without having to earn any more money than you do currently? What if you could achieve your financial goals without having to suffer deprivation?

It's easier than you think.

In Part One of this book, I will challenge some of your preconceived notions and automatic responses to money. I will debunk the myths, the rules about money that pervade our lives—such as the myth that more money will make us happier.

After questioning some of the automatic beliefs and choices you make around money, you might choose to keep right on in the same direction. However, you will have at least examined your choices.

In Part Two, I will show you a plan for saving and spending that really works. I am not talking about a "budget"—budgets don't work. I am talking about a personal spending and savings plan that puts focus on the things you value most in your life.

Nothing has a broader and more far–reaching influence on our lives than money. It represents security and survival, prestige and power, elegance, energy, and control. It represents the possibility to realize our dreams and be more helpful to others. It contains some of our greatest fears: the fear of being without, of being powerless, of not being worthy or accepted.

Money is a presence that follows us through every day of our lives. Yet our relationship to it has developed haphazardly, built upon faulty ideas, misinformation, and fears. We don't talk about it in any meaningful way—like sex, we make jokes about it and then avoid dealing with it.

Our relationship with money arises from the choices we make—yet we make many of these choices automatically. We often respond from a subliminal level.

We need to raise our awareness regarding the choices we make with money. Do our choices about money generate more frustration or more satisfaction in our lives? Do our choices give us more or less time? Do they make us feel like we are stuck on a treadmill, or do they open up possibilities we only dreamed of?

Where did we get our preconceived notions on how to spend money? How did we buy into this mandate that requires us to pay for four years of college for our kids—a $50,000 to $370,000 investment!—even when it might not be in their best interest to go to college at all? Where did we get the idea that a bigger house is always better, or that a home is a good investment? Who told us that we have to suffer through forty years of working at jobs that gradually kill us, so we can begin to live the life we want when we are sixty-five?

Most of us first learned about money from our parents—not by talking about it in any meaningful way, but by observing. But our parents may not have been the best role models in the management and spending of money. After all, they probably learned about money by observing *their* parents.

Then we spent from twelve to sixteen years of our lives in school with little or no mention of how to manage money effectively.

Now, we are bombarded by advertising that encourages us to consume more. Peer pressure influences us as we compare what we have to others, and try to keep up with them.

Yet somehow, we're expected to know how to maneuver our way through a complex and economically driven world, fraught with temptations of pricey goods, expensive lifestyle habits, and credit cards. And if we get in over our heads, with whom do we talk about it? Our friends? Our co-workers? I doubt it. We're sure that they have it handled, and we're too worried of what they'll think of us.

Money should be a tool for positive growth and possibility in our lives. It should allow us to lead more fulfilling lives and give us the opportunity to help others more. However, for most people, it does not do these things. It causes anxiety and strain instead. This stress can take many forms, from worrying about how much to buy for our kids, to spending freely on them, but never feeling good about it. It can manifest itself as a growing belief that no matter how hard we work, we'll never get ahead. Money stress can grow into anxiety about funding a realistic plan for retirement, which may even lead some people to not fund a plan at all. It can negatively influence marriage and family, spawning defensive relationships or resentment about not getting "what we deserve." Just imagine how our personal effectiveness, health, and sense of well being could be enhanced if we weren't worrying about money!

In the pages to come, I am going to ask you to take a look at your life. I'll ask you to pay attention to the attitudes and automatic beliefs you have about money, and how you use money in your life.

I want you to challenge the assumptions that keep you working at your current job. I want you to reconsider your plan to fund entirely your kids' college expenses. We will look at whether an expensive car is really worth the cost, and we'll reconsider the heart of the American Dream: that you should own a home.

I am not your typical financial planner—I want you to break the rules. By the time we're done, you will agree that "everything you know about money is wrong."

So, let's get to work.

PART I

The Money Myths

More Money Will Make Me Happier

The greatest myth is the idea that money will make us happier. And the more money we have, the happier we'll be. If we *only* had more. It is so ingrained that people don't recognize it as something they choose to believe. To challenge this premise is like questioning some sacred truth. People feel unbelievably strong about this idea, as if I am crazy even to doubt its validity.

Recently I had a holiday card made up to send out to my clients. Inside, it said, *"If money doesn't bring you happiness, what really does?"* Members of my staff came up to me and said incredulously, "But money does bring you happiness. How can you say this?"

To illustrate why money can't buy happiness, I often use the example of a very rich woman I know. A few years ago, I spoke with Annie Simpson** about her experience

---

**Clients' names and circumstances have been altered to protect their confidentiality.

with money and wealth. Annie was a millionaire many times over. She disclosed that she had inherited much of it when she was thirteen years old, following the death of her mother. Two million dollars was set aside in a trust and invested until she was twenty-one.

She told me she could jump on a Concorde and fly to Paris for lunch, return in the afternoon, and it wouldn't even cause a blip in her finances. She had so much money, it embarrassed her.

I commented on how her money must enhance the amount of free time she had.

"Enhanced? I'm afraid it has only diminished it," she said.

"How could that be?" I asked. "You don't need to spend time earning money."

"No, but I have to manage my portfolio. I have acquired properties that need attention. I have a staff to manage. The more money a person has," she said, "the more complex his or her life becomes. Having money doesn't necessarily mean that you have more time."

"But aside from that," I asked, "you must have more peace of mind, don't you?

"Do you know that I have never known the meaning of boundaries?" she replied. "I have never had to deal with limits. I'm sure you've heard the story of the young child with the fence around the yard. It is because of the fence that the child learns about security and limits. And it is by crossing the fence that the child ultimately experiences freedom. I have never had that fence. I do not know what freedom is. I do not know what security is—there's not much peace of mind without those things."

"But certainly, you are happier because you don't have to worry about money," I said.

"Consider this," she said. "When someone wants to be my friend I have to wonder if they are being nice to me because they truly like me or because they are interested in my money. I have to distrust people's intentions until they are perfectly clear. This is not the most fertile ground for sincere and lasting relationships. Wouldn't you agree?"

Annie looked out the window of my office to the trees in front. "You know, when you have this much money, you don't even get to have a bad day," she said.

I asked her to explain.

"When I am feeling lonely or low and I call up a friend, they immediately say, "Jeez, how can you have problems—you have so much money." They won't even allow me to go into it. They figure that all their problems are related to money. And since I have a lot of money, I must not have problems. I don't even get permission to have them!"

Annie was the richest person I had ever talked to. Even though part of me thought she was just spoiled and ungrateful, I could see she was also one of the most miserable people I had ever met.

I realize that most people reading this book have less money than Annie Simpson does, and that she represents an extreme example. But I tell her story because her experience flies so clearly in the face of the myth that *money buys happiness.*

Take a look at the lives of many of the world's rich and famous people and you often see a repeating pattern of broken marriages, drug or alcohol problems, and deep discontent. We all know people who have more money than we do: money for travel, more fashionable clothes, or bigger cars. But are they really happier than we are? We are so conditioned to think that money is the solution that we idolize and emulate people who have lots of it. We continue to lust after what they have.

Freedom, time, peace, happiness, and security—these are qualities dear to our souls. We all yearn for them, but their existence is not dependent upon money. They are not derived from the outside world.

More money will not solve your problems. Ultimately, it will *not* make you happier. What makes you happier comes from within.

Are you happier than you were three years ago? Aren't you making more money now? Surely you've increased your earning potential since college. Do you remember saying back then, "If I had this much money, I'd have it made?" You've probably made that much by now. Has it really increased your freedom, time, peace, happiness, or security?

Of course, I am assuming that your basic survival needs are being met—that you have more than the minimal funds necessary to support your existence. When I speak of having more money, I mean that imagined state where you could finally say, "Now I've made it. Now I'm happy."

Step back for a moment. What *does* bring you happiness? Is it playing with your kids? Taking a stroll in the woods? Listening to beautiful music? Do you do these things enough? If not, it's not a lack of money that keeps you from doing them, but a misguided priority system.

Our culture has at its core the idea that more is better. Many of us design our lives around this belief. And yet the underlying qualities that truly affect happiness are not advanced one whit by having more material things. More peace of mind is gained by allowing ourselves to be satisfied with what we already have. More joy is not bought; it is found in our hearts.

In personal financial management, the place to begin is to adopt a realistic perspective. Money will only improve the quality of your life when it is used with clarity. Only when you learn to spend money in concert with your underlying values—the things that you most deeply care about—will it become a tool for creating a more fulfilling life.

But you can't come to that conclusion unless you *talk* about money. So let's begin by attacking the myth that says we aren't supposed to.

I Can't Talk About Money

Whenever I give a speech or teach a class, I ask the audience, "How many of you feel that everyone besides you has money figured out? That your co-workers, neighbors or friends know more than you do?" Without fail, hands fly up across the room.

Each of us harbors the deep belief that he or she is the only one who is screwed up about money. Everyone else has it all figured out—they have all the things they need and never spend more than they make. We are sure that they must have a fully-funded retirement plan and a lucrative investment portfolio. They certainly understand what a 401(k) plan is, and they have just the right amount of insurance for their needs. They can't be over their heads in credit card debt like we are. We see many of them leading affluent lifestyles, which serves as evidence that all these beliefs are true.

Since we believe that other people know more than we do, we don't talk about money. We don't want to expose our ignorance. We are like the teenager afraid to talk about sex or understand it in a meaningful way. We feel that everyone else at school knows more than we do. So we pretend to know, hoping somewhere along the line that we will learn the secret. And everyone else around us pretends to know, too.

At parties, we talk about the latest hot stock or give an opinion about the real estate market. We might even brag about the high return we're getting on our investments. But if our checkbook hasn't been balanced in two years, or if our paycheck is spent three days before receiving it, then these conversations leave us uneasy. Underneath, we feel inadequate. But we keep on, not mentioning our concerns to anyone, because—somehow—we are supposed to know all about money.

The problem is that if we don't talk to people about our financial issues or our money problems, then we will do the same thing month after month, always hoping it will turn out differently. Rita Mae Brown defined insanity as "doing the same thing over and over and expecting a different result." In the arena of money, many of us fit her definition of insanity.

We get most of this programming from our families. Most of us never really talked about money when we were growing up. In seminar after seminar, I ask, "What did your parents say about money?" Invariably, someone in the group says, "Nothing."

Money was taboo. It wasn't a thing you talked about. For some unknown reason never explained, money was a "hush-hush" subject.

This is not to say we didn't receive clear messages. In most cases, we did:

"There's not enough."

"You have to work hard to earn money."

"We can't because we can't afford it."

Or if Mom and Dad paid for everything, then the message may have been:

"Don't think about it, someone else will take care of you."
And later in life we wonder why it all didn't turn out that way.

Simply put, we never had a chance to really learn about money. At the dinner table our parents may have asked us about our day in school, or how we felt about getting a new puppy, or where we wanted to go on vacation. But no one ever said, "Okay, let's talk about money."

This silence surrounding money was further reinforced by a school system that rarely, if ever, brought up the subject. We were not taught about home finances, investing, or the basics of financial planning, or retirement planning.

So we're supposed to know about money—*but we've never been taught.* Imagine going down to the driver's license office and taking our driving test without ever having been taught how to drive.

We can't hide bad driving skills for too long. But we have gotten highly skilled in masking our ignorance over money. We "compare and despair." We look at other people and grade ourselves based upon how we perceive we are doing financially versus them.

Money has become synonymous with personal identity and self-worth. If we don't have enough money, then we feel we aren't good enough. We don't talk to people about money because we are worried that we don't have as much as they do. And if we think we have more than they do, then we don't talk about it because we don't want them to feel uncomfortable. We believe people wouldn't like us if they knew the truth.

We generally believe that other people are more on track, in better shape than we are financially. We keep up a good outer appearance and hope no one brings up the subject.

Work is a great place for this acting job. We fear that if our co-workers knew the truth—that we don't have money figured out—that they would raise doubts about our ability to do our jobs.

What would our bosses think if they knew we haven't balanced our checkbooks in two years, we are over our heads in credit card debt, and we don't understand the difference between a money market and a mutual fund? If our job is to balance the department's budget, what would they think if they knew we couldn't manage our own personal finances?

Mary McAfferty, a client of mine in her mid-thirties, managed a $1.5 million budget at work. She consistently received bonuses, pay increases, and promotions for doing such a brilliant job.

At home, she hadn't balanced her checkbook in a year. Each month, she was spending $1,500 more than she made. She practiced retail therapy. If she had a bad day, she compensated by buying new clothes or going out for an expensive dinner. Emotion drove her personal spending habits.

At work, on the other hand, she based her decisions on responsible and rational thinking.

Mary hadn't told anybody about her personal financial situation until she finally gathered the courage to see me. Together, we started to address her money problems. She faced the fact that if she didn't do something about them, her financial future would remain forever unstable.

Mary had to overcome a great deal of embarrassment to make the appointment to see me. She felt she was somehow dumber about money than the people around her. She thought she was too old to be having these kinds of problems—that it would be an admission of ignorance to talk to someone. She feared that if she did so, her abilities on the job would be questioned. But her willingness to talk to someone meaningfully about money reduced her stress, and she began to turn her financial ship in the right direction.

In talking with her, it became clear that she didn't have a clue about where her money went, so the first thing we did was to list everything she spent. Then we determined what her top financial goals were and how much it would cost to attain them. She decided how she was going to change her spending habits to stop spending more than she was making and to achieve her financial goals. By talking about her situation, she was able to get over her embarrassment and hopelessness. Only then could she get the coaching she needed to change how she operated with her personal finances.

She stopped spending more than she made and started an investment portfolio. She started to feel she was as much on top of her personal finances as she was in control of the company's budget at work.

Another client, Lisa Pasco, is a teacher. She belongs to the Washington State Teacher's Retirement System, which offers their members nearly thirty different options to use for retirement tax shelters. It's overwhelming. Lisa knew she should be saving more for retirement, but she didn't know where to start. She didn't know how to evaluate an investment, and she was afraid she would buy into a bad one. She kept letting the years go by, knowing that she should do something, but not knowing which way to turn. She was afraid to talk to anyone about it.

She waited until she was 49 years old to come in and see me. By not talking to anyone, and therefore not contributing to her retirement sooner, she had lost years of appreciation. I evaluated the thirty options for her and she finally set up an annuity. She was regretful she had not done anything earlier, but had been too embarrassed to take the first step and ask anyone about it.

If you are confused or intimidated or frustrated about money, the place to start is to realize that you need to find someone you can talk to about it.

Who is this someone? If you are concerned that your finances are not heading in the right direction, it may be time to seek out a professional. If you work for a company that has a benefits department, talk to them about your retirement options. Tell them you do not understand the brochures or written explanations of the plans. Tell them that you really don't know anything about investments, that you need answers to some basic questions about your options. *Tell them you need help.* Ask them to work with you until you do understand.

In my experience, any time you start a conversation like that, people will be more than willing to help you.

A financial planner is another source to consult for advice. Ask friends, co-workers, or people in your human resource department if they can give you a referral.

You need to talk to someone with whom you are comfortable. If the person leaves you feeling like you should know all of this stuff already, then that is not the person for you.

A 41-year-old self-employed client of mine decided to set up a retirement plan. He requested information from a company offering a wide range of options. He decided how much a month he could invest, filled out the forms, and sent them in. He received another packet of information in the mail, and soon afterwards, a third. Inside were plans, brochures, and a video. There were five different forms to fill out. He tried to work through the maze, but he was left confused and overwhelmed.

He called the company's 800 number for help. When he expressed his confusion, the "personal account specialist" told him, "Well, you need to wade through the information." He protested that he had done that and still was confused. He needed help knowing which forms to fill out. The specialist again told him to just go through the information and he would understand.

He hung up angry and lost. He continued to put off starting a plan because the attitude of the "specialist" made him feel dumb.

Customer service representatives deal with this information all the time. They sometimes seem incredulous that you do not know everything there is to know about Roth IRAs, 401(k) plans, annuities, SEPs, and growth versus income funds. When you have one or two intimidating interactions, it reinforces the belief that everyone knows about and understands this money stuff—everyone, that is, except you.

Shop around for a Certified Financial Planner who is willing to listen to you and who takes the time to understand your concerns, fears, and goals. You want someone who will work with you to alleviate your financial troubles and help you to establish a personal spending plan, a set of financial goals, and an investment and retirement plan with which you are comfortable, and that you fully understand.

An important distinction to note is that between *fee-only* and *commission-based* financial planners. Fee-only Certified Financial Planners charge you an agreed upon fee for consultation or a flat fee for services rendered. If they are managing your investments, they will charge a percentage of assets under management. They do not have a vested interest in anything they recommend to you. (To locate a fee-only financial planner in your area, see Appendix page 191.)

Commission-based financial planners, on the other hand, receive a commission on what they sell. This arrangement can create a conflict of interest. A planner may recommend to you an investment or an insurance policy even if it isn't in your best interest—just because that is the only way he or she will be compensated. You may very well find a great advisor who is a commission-based planner. Just be aware of the potential conflict of interest.

The most important thing is that a financial planner

should be a trusted and objective counselor. Choose someone you can talk to easily and who will charge you based on a compensation arrangement that feels comfortable.

Find someone you can trust to advise you and start talking about money. As with anything that is challenging, talking and learning about it will help reduce stress and get you started on the right track.

I Don't Like My Job but I Can't Afford to Leave It

Bill Patrick sat in my office, his knuckles white from grasping the arms of his chair.

"I only have to make it through twelve more years, and then I am eligible for early retirement," he said. Bill worked for a government agency and hated it. He was 43 years old.

"Twelve years!" I said, "That's a lot of time. Are you going to make it?"

"I think so," he said. "At least I think I will. I mean, I'll have my retirement income then."

We did an analysis on Bill's retirement plan and his future financial needs at age 55. They didn't add up. The plan was not going to provide him enough money for the lifestyle he desired when he left the work world.

To provide for his wife and himself at retirement, Bill was going to have to work more than the twelve years he had planned. Not surprisingly, this news was about as welcome as a storm cloud at a picnic.

"What can I do?" he asked.

"Look," I said. "Twelve years is a long time, and it's going to take even longer than that before you can realistically retire. For you, it's going to feel like an especially long time because you hate your job. I'm guessing that it's not the length of time you dread, it's the prospect of spending the next twelve years doing something you do not want to do."

"I don't have any choice," he said.

"What about doing work that you like?" I asked. "Since it's going to take you longer to get to retirement than you hoped, you might as well do something you enjoy."

Bill's situation is true for many people—their retirement funding is not going to be adequate. Pension plans are no longer guaranteed, benefits are continuously being scaled back, and people are losing their jobs to corporate downsizing. What our parents took as a given—namely, that the company would take care of us—is rarely even in the realm of possibility today.

Add the fact that the cost of living continues to rise, and it becomes clear that most of us will have to work longer than we thought before we can retire. The time will not seem as long, however, if you spend it doing something you like to do or work with people you enjoy.

I am not just saying "follow your bliss, the money will follow." While this might happen, to go blindly in pursuit of a business or career scheme based on unrealistic expectations can be financially disastrous and cause as much—if not more—stress than staying at a job you dislike. Most of us have other people in our lives who are at least partially, if not wholly, dependent upon us to earn money.

We do need, however, to dispel this notion that we just need to struggle through a few more years and then we'll have it made—retirement at last! Just one more day with our jaws clenched and bodies stressed, and then we'll be there. Then another day, and then another. . .

We finally make it to the weekend for a little relief (maybe!). Then we get up Monday morning only to jump on the hamster wheel again.

You will be more likely to find an alternative to a crummy job if you are open and receptive to the possibility. Then you have to *do* something about it. Just working and complaining doesn't get you anywhere.

I asked Bill, "Okay, what are you really passionate about? What do you think about most? What excites you?"

"Chess," he replied.

"Chess?"

"Yes. It's what I love to do most. I read about it. I play it. I go to tournaments."

We explored ways that Bill might turn his passion into real income. Obviously, we were not going to replace his $45,000 job with income from chess activities—at least not right away. But we played with a number of ideas. Could he author a book about chess? How about a CD-ROM? Could he organize chess tournaments and invite big name players?

Bill didn't waste time. Since our meeting, he has organized a number of local chess tournaments and is even beginning to see a little income flow from this activity. Who knows where it might lead him from here? And even if his income from these activities is never substantial, by doing what he loves, the time until he can retire will not seem so much like a prison sentence.

Even if your search doesn't lead to work you love, it helps to find people with whom you like to work, feel a connection, and like to be around.

Aaron Wilson tried out many different careers in his life, from sales to manufacturing to teaching, but he found them unfulfilling. He felt like something must be wrong with him to be in his forties and still not able to find work that he loved doing. Finally, he came to terms with the fact that work was not the main passion in his life. Developing a spiritual life became more central to him, and work became a secondary concern. He became committed to finding a group of people who shared his values and to whom he could relate. He now works as a financial analyst in a small firm with people he truly enjoys. Now, going to work is a source of satisfaction in his life. The people he works with make the difference.

Each of the following clients has something in common. They had grown progressively dissatisfied with the status quo, of working in a career that did not fulfill them. They identified an interest they wanted to follow, and then they became motivated to change. Finally, they worked up the courage to take steps to manifest this change in the world. They moved into more fulfilling work.

Marcie worked for a major law firm. She was upwardly mobile, working fifteen hours a day, but she didn't feel like she was a part of the firm's soul. She wasn't even sure it had one. We discussed some alternatives. Eventually, she went on to start—and now runs—a non-profit corporation that teaches computer literacy to inner-city kids.

Charley Silverstein owns a very successful medical supply company that distributes to major hospitals in the Pacific Northwest. Whenever I asked him about his work, he seemed embarrassed and didn't want to talk about it.

But he loves to make wine. Mention wine and he becomes completely animated. When he brings out his Pinot Noir and his Chardonnay and starts talking about next year's crop and where he is going to travel to buy the grapes, his eyes light up. He's mad about wine and winemaking.

Charley is in the process of making a transition from his career in medical supplies to one in winemaking. Will he make as much money? Probably not, at least at first. But he comes alive when he's involved in making wine.

Jackie Canterbury was a teacher at a private middle school. Everyone loved her—kids, their parents, her fellow teachers. But she had done it for so long that the challenge was no longer there. Increasingly, she found herself just going through the motions. She left that job and joined forces with her partner, an artist. Together, they started to expand their art business. It has been three years since she left her teaching job, and her income is now higher than it was as a teacher, and going to work is a joy.

We have been conditioned to think of work as a burden. How many people do you know who visibly light up when they talk about their work? Well, they should. We all should. If we fail this simple test, maybe it's a sign that we need to explore other avenues of work.

It is not a farfetched idea to simply find something you like doing, with people you like to be around, and have that become your life's work. You can begin slowly. You can make the transition step by step from what you are currently doing to something you like more.

Don't put it off—you have no idea where it might lead.

Remember that the need to earn money is not the cause of the problem. The problem is in believing that the *only* way to earn enough money is to continue doing something you dislike, and that you have to stay at that job until you retire because of financial concerns. Unfortunately, retirement may be a long time in coming.

The greatest rationalization out there for staying with a

job that is not fulfilling is the statement, "Well, the money is good." It is true that you may temporarily experience a drop in income when you leave a job to do something you love. It takes a while to become established in a new career or business. However, many of my clients who have switched to more fulfilling careers have also increased their earnings. Don't automatically assume you will make less money at something you like doing. By willingly throwing your heart, soul, and overtime into your new career, your likelihood for success will greatly increase. But even if you never make as much money in your new career, you may well find that the increase in personal satisfaction more than makes up for the lost income.

You will need to commit to a plan to make the transition successful. You might have to save up a fund to get you through the start-up phase. You might have to watch your spending habits extra closely during this time or continue working part time in your old job while you slowly begin to activate your new career. Your spouse may have to work full-time while you make the transition. It may take lots of work and time, but it won't happen until you take the first step.

Quit your job? You bet. A lot can happen in the next twelve or fifteen years. *Start now.*

MYTH #4

I Can't Buy or Do Something because I Don't Have the Money

I started setting financial goals for myself at an early age. I grew up on a farm in the country seven miles from Loveland, Colorado. I didn't have neighborhood kids to play with, so I had to generate my own entertainment. At the ripe old age of nine, I decided to buy a stereo. Most normal nine-year-old kids spent their money on candy and comic books. But to me, a stereo meant companionship, so nothing was going to stop me.

Without knowing it, I was zeroing in on a key to personal financial well-being: *Be clear about what you want.*

I was determined. I even knew which stereo I wanted: I saw it in the appliance store where my mom bought her washer. It had a receiver, a turntable, an 8-track player (I know, I'm dating myself) and the best part of all, the speakers. They looked like sleek end tables with slate black tops. No matter where you were in the room, the sound was aimed at you. It was cool.

My only sources of income were my $2-a-week allowance and the occasional money I received as gifts. I saved for over a year. I didn't spend a dime. For birthdays and holidays, I always asked for money.

At long last I had the $163 saved to buy that cool stereo with the awesome speakers!

I'll never forget the day when we went to the appliance store. My mom told the salesman I wanted to buy a stereo. He asked me which one and I pointed to it. He then asked my mom how she was going to pay for it. She said, "I'm not buying it; she is." His eyes popped out as I brought out my wad of carefully folded $1, $5, and $10 bills.

Early on I learned the joy and power of setting and achieving financial goals. I learned the power of "I can!"

When faced with a desire to do or buy something we've always wanted, most of us make a quick review of our mental checkbook and say, "Oh, I don't have the money." We make this assessment quickly and automatically. The door slams shut. I've seen it time and again when I ask people why they don't do something they really want to do. "Why don't you go ahead and go to Hawaii? You've wanted to do it for years." In the vast majority of cases, the answer comes out in no time, "Oh, I can't afford it."

I generally prescribe a much more constructive and positive approach. I have people ask themselves, "If this is something that is really important to me—that I really value, and very much want to do—then how can I make it work? How does it fit into my current goals? If it looks like this new thing may be more important than a goal I previously had, then maybe I can free up the resources to accomplish this new goal."

An acquaintance told me recently about the laser surgery he had on his eyes. He had put it off for years because he thought he couldn't afford it. After finally getting it done, he told me, "If I had known how great it was going to be, I would have done this long ago."

One of my clients, Norman Benson, found out that Bob Dylan and Van Morrison were playing together in a New York City concert. He had been a long-time Dylan fan, and for years had wanted to see Van Morrison. But Norman lived in Seattle. It just wasn't practical. There were expenses that included airfare, hotel, food, and concert tickets. It was crazy just to think about it. But he couldn't stop thinking about it. It made an especially strong impression on him that the concert was to be on his 40th birthday.

He was taking a walk around a lake in a local park, and he kept fantasizing about being at the show. He didn't know how he was going to afford it. He stopped walking and asked himself a question, "Six months from now, what will I wish I had done?" The answer was immediate. He made some changes in his spending habits and found a way to afford it. Norman Benson was going to the concert.

A few years ago, I decided to go to China to adopt a

baby. The trip would take about ten days. I needed a travel companion. I asked a friend of mine who is a seasoned traveler to accompany me. She'd know what food to eat and what not to drink. She had experience in other cultures where English is rarely spoken. She would not be intimidated by traveling in China, as I might be.

As a successful stockbroker, I knew that she could afford it. I called her and asked her if she would consider coming with me. Immediately, her reaction was, "No—I can't—I can't leave my business for that long . . . I don't think that would work."

A week later, she called me back. She broke into tears and said, "I asked my business partner (her husband) if I could go. He said, 'If you want to go, go!' And then I thought, when I'm sixty-five, what will I say to myself? 'Oh yeah, I'm really glad I didn't go to China with Karen because I got to work for two more weeks.'"

She came with me. We had the time of our lives. And the relationship she now has with my daughter is priceless.

If there is something you deeply want to do, you can find a way. You *can* afford it.

When faced with the challenge of a new goal, our immediate reaction is usually, "I haven't saved for it. I can't do that."

Saying "No, I don't have the money" is just an excuse. It's an easy out. When we say that, we don't have to confront what it will take to accomplish the goal.

It also lets us off the hook with other people. We know that saying, "I can't afford it" is a socially acceptable excuse for not going for it. Hopefully, our real friends will see through our objection and tell us, "If you really want to go, you'll find a way. Do it!" And they should—we all need a little prodding occasionally.

Unfortunately, we are all too often polite. We don't want to make waves around money issues. So the next time a friend tells you that he or she can't follow a dream because he or she doesn't have the money—don't buy into it!

You have options. If there's something you really want, do a little brainstorming and make some choices. Maybe you don't need to get that new living room furniture this year if it means you will be able to take that dream vacation instead. Maybe you don't have to go out to dinner every week for the next six months if it means being able to take that art class you've always wanted to take. Maybe you don't have to spend $1,000 on presents this holiday season if you can get out of debt instead. Maybe you don't need to go to the Nordstrom's sale if you can instead fly your sister in from Baltimore to attend the family reunion.

You have possibilities. But to access them you need to allow yourself to overcome the automatic response that says, "I can't."

Instead, try "I can." If you allow yourself to see your wish as a potential reality, you can begin the constructive process of taking small steps in that direction. You can begin working on the "how," and begin to solve the problems between you and your goal.

Ask yourself, "Six months from now, a year from now, three years from now, what will I wish I had done?" Look at your life right now. What are those things that you are most proud of accomplishing? The trip to Greece? The 1957 T-bird you finally bought? The little independent theater production you produced? I bet these were the very things that at first blush you didn't think you could do because of money. But these are the things you found a way to achieve. They were goals you consciously chose and successfully pursued.

One should use discretion here. I am not suggesting you go hog wild pursuing anything and everything you might want. But if it is something very special that calls to you deeply, then find a way to bring it into your life.

In many cases, the financial resources for something you sincerely desire do not materialize until you commit to it. I have seen this countless times in my own life and in the lives of my clients. Doors with resources behind them opened only after the commitment was made.

So go. Do it! Commit! If there's something you want, say, "I can." Then find a way to make it happen.

I Have to Pay for My Kids' College Education

Most clients who come through my door consider it a given that they have to fully fund their children's college education for four years. It's a ton of money. And for a lot of kids, it's neither what they want to do nor what is best for them.

For those who do want to go to college, allowing them to share in the cost actually prepares them to be more responsible later in life. It also gives them the incentive to discover in school what they really want to do instead of just getting a degree to please their parents.

Many baby boomers had all or most of their college education paid for. It was not even open to debate. One client told me his parents said, "It's not a question of whether you will go to college, but what college you will go to."

This "I have to pay for the kids' college" mandate is so strong that people are shocked when I question it. When I show them the financial implications of this mandate, their eyes roll back in their heads.

A couple who begins saving for a college education for their ten-year-old child will have to put away $650 to $700 a month for eight years for their child to attend a typical in-state public school, and $2,000 a month for eight years to attend a private one. Even if a couple begins saving when the child is born, the monthly bill is still on average $216 for an in-state public school and $460 for a private college, each month, for eighteen years. And this is per child!

We love our children and of course we want the best for them. But we automatically make this mental leap that the best thing for them is to go to college. We assume that to be a good parent means we must pay for all of it. We certainly don't want our kids going around telling their friends, "Well, my parents aren't going to pay for my college." What would the neighbors think?

Where is it written that we have to pay for our kids' entire college education? Where is it written that we are bad parents if we don't?

You *don't* have to pay for four years (or more) of your child's college. Financial planning is about peace of mind, not the avoidance of guilt.

I am certainly not saying that college is bad. Far from it. For thousands, if not millions of people, it is a valuable experience. But I am drawing attention to the automatic assumption that you have to pay for it, and at the institution of your child's choice, and for as long as they want to go there.

Because of the automatic belief that parents must pay for college, most parents do not involve their kids in the decision-making process of how it will be paid for.

I want my daughters to go to college, but I want them to pay for part of it. I want them to generate the will power, the interest, and the drive to do what it takes to make it happen. I am already beginning to talk to my seven-year-old daughter, Marie, about the choices she will have in her future. I tell her I will help her in accomplishing what she wants, but that *she* has to be the driving force. It will be a family effort, but it must be propelled by her desire.

Not only is the cost of a college education rising at least 5% a year, but there is another disturbing trend afoot. Even if you have systematically saved the $50,000–$370,000 for tuition, it is becoming increasingly unlikely your child will be admitted to the college of his or her choice, especially if it is an upper echelon one. So if saving for your child's college education means you must sacrifice all your other financial goals, you may want to rethink your plan.

Dave Love, a client of mine, sent his daughter to the most prestigious private high school in San Francisco with the intent that she would have an advantage getting into Stanford or an equivalent elite college. This high school was very difficult academically. A 3.5 GPA at this school is equivalent to a 4.0 in most public high schools. His daughter had earned a 3.5 GPA, had done things to bolster her education on her summer vacations, and had excelled in extracurricular activities. He and his wife have had their hearts set on this goal. They have been saving an enormous amount of money annually for the last ten years to be able to send their daughter to Stanford. They have regularly sacrificed other things in order to realize this dream, such as trips abroad and improvements to their home.

Recently, they met with her counselor. They were told, "Your daughter won't get into Stanford." Dave was shocked. When he protested, the counselor rattled off the names of numerous students with 4.0 averages and exceptional citizenship and extracurricular accomplishments who had not been accepted.

There are so many baby boomers with so many kids who have excelled academically that the likelihood of our children getting into the elite schools is down there with the chance of an excellent high school basketball player making it into the NBA.

While considering this, you must also ask yourself: *What is best for my child?*

Doug Francis, a client of mine, had paid a considerable amount of money to send his son to an elite film school. The family has had to live under a tremendous debt in order to pay this expense. Doug followed a similar plan for his daughter and made the same commitment to her. He and his wife worked to exhaustion to make it happen. They moved her to New York, set her up in an apartment, and registered her for art school.

She came home four months later and told them it was torture. It was not working. After one quarter, she dropped out. She wasn't able to perform at the college curriculum level. It wasn't what she wanted to do. After some soul searching, she had decided she wants to work as a guide in wilderness education. Years of work and deprivation and emotional stress went toward fulfilling this mandate to send their daughter to college, and it was not what was best for her in the long run.

Sometimes this insistence to pay for our kids' college education can set them further back than ahead.

Duncan Cresent's parents paid for four years of his college. But it was understood that what he was to get out of college was a degree in a responsible profession—which meant a money-making profession. This highly creative individual became an accountant. It took him many years working for CPA firms and in the business world to uncover his true vocation and talent as a writer. All those years he had veered from his true path out of a deep-rooted desire to please his parents. After all, they paid for his college education.

His parents meant well. They wanted the best for him. But they were operating from automatic beliefs—that he should go to college, that he should become degreed in a responsible profession, and that they should pay for it. He was never involved in the decision. He was to succeed. He was to achieve.

If Duncan's parents had allowed him to invest in this decision both psychologically and financially, it might have awakened him sooner to his natural vocation—writing. In his case, a liberal arts degree with time out for some travel would have made much more sense than an accounting degree.

Step back and ask yourself if college is the best place for your children to express themselves at their highest ability and greatest fulfillment. Is your automatic decision to spend a fortune on four or more years of college based on what is *truly* best for them, or is it based on what you *assume* is best for them? Do you really need to fall prey to this automatic decision to pay for four or more years of college? After all, who is this unique individual who is your daughter or son? How can you help shape and mold them in ways that will assist them to become fully expressive in their lives? Does that include college or are there other things you should be investigating?

Some kids are better served by going to a junior college or a trade school. Some kids are better served attending school overseas, or entering the Peace Corps, or starting work and gaining some experience first. If your child has always dreamed of making films, then a specialized one-year film program may be just what she needs.

When they graduate from high school, kids are only

seventeen or eighteen years old. Maybe they need a chance to develop a bit more emotionally before committing to a career and a very expensive college. Some need a chance to discover more of their true interests. It takes considerable grace and wisdom for parents to promote such development.

Since the investment in college is so large today, you can help your children by allowing them to participate in the decision and the economic cost. Talk to them about the issue when they are in sixth grade, in junior high, and in high school. Allow them to take more responsibility over their long-term lives. Work with them to discover what they really want to do. Help them understand what it will cost to attend a college in-state versus out-of-state, or the cost of learning a vocational skill, or studying overseas. How much will they have to earn or borrow beyond what you are willing to contribute? If they decide to take out a loan, then they need to understand what it will take to pay it off. Perhaps this will allow them to gain some life experience that will be as valuable a part of their college education as the degree they earn.

Dick Buell is a 34-year-old attorney who works for one of the most prestigious law firms in Portland. He had to put himself through college, and he graduated with about $50,000 in student loans.

He told me, "When I was attending school, I took care of business. Because I was paying for it, getting good grades was a very high priority for me. Plus I had to use my time wisely to fit in enough time for studying around my work schedule. While I was working, my buddies—whose parents were footing their college bills—were hanging out at the local tavern in the afternoon or watching TV. Most of them didn't study much and weren't at all clear about why they were in college in the first place."

Dick told me that his student loan is down to $7,500 and should be paid off before the end of the year. "It's been a long journey," he said, "but it's almost done. And I'll tell you—when I get it paid off, you won't find anyone prouder."

When kids participate in paying for their college expenses, they receive a valuable life lesson. It helps them in the long run by making them more aware of finances and what it takes to accomplish a financial goal. It allows them to be more responsible and share in the reward of fulfilling a financial obligation. And it might motivate them to find out more about what they want to do in life.

We are a generation that is petrified by the thought of denying our children anything. We believe that giving them everything is the way to be good parents. It doesn't work. They don't learn responsibility, and this accommodating environment doesn't always support them in discovering their own abiding passions. We must accept the fact that it's okay to let them work at it a bit.

When confronting the cost of fully funding a college

education for their kids today, a lot of people are coming to the conclusion that they just don't have enough to do it. Perhaps that's okay. And even if you do have enough money, it's still okay to question the whole idea.

Now, let me be clear. It's still fine to pay for your kids' college if you choose to. But you can reflect on it first instead of automatically thinking that you *have to* pay for it.

When it comes to one of the biggest financial obligations of your life—your kids' college costs—there are alternatives. Explore them.

I Should Buy a Home because It's a Great Investment

When I do a retirement projection for a client, I always put together an evaluation of his or her total investments. Nearly every client says to me, "Just a minute! You forgot something. You didn't include my house."

I say, "That's true. I didn't include your house. Your house is a roof over your head. *It's not an investment.*"

When I told this fact to one couple, they looked surprised. "But it's a two bedroom rambler," the wife protested. "And it's in a nice neighborhood. Its assessed value has risen steadily for the past six years. How can you say it's not an investment?"

"Do you plan on continuing to live there?" I asked.

"Yes. We're not moving any time soon."

"Then unless you plan on ultimately selling it and then

downsizing to a smaller, less expensive house—and living off the proceeds of the gain—it is not an investment. It's just a roof over your head."

Some clients say they plan to live in their house for about five years, then sell it and buy another house. That's fine, but if the real estate market has risen increasing the value of your home, then the prices of all the other homes in the area have risen, as well. Your gain will be swallowed up by the increased price of your new home. You will not be getting ahead.

You buy a house for $150,000 and ten years later you sell it for $300,000. On paper, it looks like you've made a lot of money, but not if your next house has appreciated, as well. The only way you will realize an investment gain is to sell, then downsize to a less expensive home or live in a rental and invest your profits from the sale.

Some clients tell me that they do intend to downsize—especially after the kids graduate from high school. But few truly do so when the time comes. Or if they do, depending on where they want to move, they find that even a smaller house is as expensive as the larger one they currently own. Smaller does not necessarily mean less expensive. Land costs may be more expensive in a new area or the new home may be outfitted with expensive extras, such as an outdoor whirlpool or higher-grade appliances and cabinets.

A couple who came to me for counseling had always planned to move back to California after their kids graduated from high school. They wanted to sell their home, a large multi-bedroom house in an upscale Seattle neighborhood. They intended to find a smaller home in a warmer climate.

"What kind of house are you looking for?" I asked.

"Well," the wife said, "one of those really nice beachfront condos."

I talked to them for awhile and asked them how large this place might be. Did the husband need an area for an office? How about a two-car garage? Did the wife want a garden? When we researched how much such a place might cost them, it turned out to be greater than the value of their current home.

We have this notion that when we retire we'll downsize and live in a smaller place—that things will be different. We'll find that little paradise cottage on the ocean or in the mountains and have all this excess money to live on from the sale of our old house.

Far too late, we find out that reality is very different.

Another factor that works against downsizing is that people have grown accustomed to a certain standard of living. The truth is, they aren't willing to sacrifice this standard of living after retirement. Time after time, my clients stay in the home they lived in for years. Or they buy something of comparable cost elsewhere.

Ask yourself what it will *really* be like after retirement. What kind of a lifestyle will you be living? Will you truly be willing to live with less, or is your vision romantically tinged? Romance is fine. I'm all for it. But, if you are basing your financial future on it, watch out. I'm not suggesting that you give up your dream. You can have it if you plan for it, but be realistic. Many of my recently retired clients report they are spending more money than they thought they would—or planned to.

A couple I know has an enormous home with multiple bedrooms, a three-car garage, and a large yard. Their kids have left for college. So now there are only two people living in this huge house, which has appreciated nearly $150,000 since they bought it. The husband, 52, is a retired legislator who now has a full-time job in private industry.

They could easily sell the home, find a smaller place and realize a six-figure gain. But the husband wants a large garage for his racing boats and for a shop. The wife wants a big yard and wants to live in an upscale neighborhood. Add it all up and you have a couple that is not going to realize a gain from the sale of their current home. They are unwilling to shift to a simpler and less expensive lifestyle.

Many of us could live in a smaller and less expensive home *right now*. But it seems ingrained in our culture that we must move from a large to an even larger home—otherwise, we're not really getting ahead.

We forget that we are buying into more than just a bigger house. The real estate taxes are more, the insurance is more. It costs more to heat it, to light it, and to maintain it.

Mortgage costs are higher. It takes more after-tax income on a monthly basis to maintain a larger house, so we have to work harder to keep up with the expenses. The extra work usually means less time available to enjoy the very home we are working to buy.

Even if you were buying a home as an investment, real estate tends to go through boom and bust cycles. The Pacific Northwest, for instance, is currently experiencing a boom. It is common these days for homes to go to the highest bidder on the first day, for higher than the asking price. It's easy to get caught up in this excitement, joining the rush to "invest" in this hot market—to jump on the runaway train before it gets away from you forever.

But is real estate a good investment?

Just look at former real estate boom areas such as Texas, Southern California, or New England. People in those areas have had to confront the fact that their house has not been a good investment. In many cases, their home has depreciated considerably in value since they bought it. Imagine living in your home for years, and then selling for a price that is less than the remaining balance on your mortgage. You would have to pay money just to get out of it!

Sometimes, people find they can't sell their house for a long time after they place it on the market, or they can't sell it at all. A client moved to Seattle from Washington, DC. Originally, the house she had left in DC was by all appearances a great place to have bought a home. It's located close to the government office buildings and in sight of the Washington Monument. But the neighborhood has "transitioned" the wrong way—toward deterioration rather than renovation. Now she can't sell her house for what it cost, and she has to rent it out to keep up the payments.

In boom times, we don't like to think about the possibility that the market may one day fall. We don't like to think about the possibility that we may not recover what we paid for our home originally, or that we won't be able to sell it at all. But it happens.

We hear stories of people who made a killing in real estate. In a lot of cases, they entered the real estate market as a business, buying and selling rental homes or buildings. But most of us are in the situation of owning just our principal residence. For us, selling and moving to a new residence is not a moneymaking endeavor—it is a move to a new home.

Some people do realize a gain from the sale of their principal residence if they then move to an area where real estate is less expensive. For instance, I know a couple who sold their California home and bought a twelve-acre spread in Montana, and they still had money to spare. But such a move involves a lifestyle choice as well as a financial one. Moving to a rural area often entails a loss of access to amenities and cultural opportunities that people in urban settings usually enjoy and take for granted.

Another factor people tend to forget is the cost of buying and selling. In the Pacific Northwest, it usually costs 1.5% of the cost of the house to buy a home and 10% to sell it. So your home has to appreciate 11.5% just to *break even*.

I also want to debunk the often-heard, "I bought a house so I could get the tax write-off." People justify their home as a good investment because they get a tax write-off for interest and real estate taxes.

They forget that it is not a dollar for dollar deduction. For instance, if you are in a 28% tax bracket and you spend a dollar on mortgage interest, you will get 28 cents back in tax savings. Paying a dollar to end up with 28 cents is not good financial planning.

A tax write-off for a home is no reason to buy.

Of course, you need a roof over your head. Buy a house in an area you want to live. Buy a home you can afford. Don't rationalize your decision to buy a more expensive home because you think it is a good investment or because it is a good tax write-off. Unless you intend to sell it eventually, and then downsize or rent a home and live off the gain, its increase in value is irrelevant. The only thing you gain in the meantime is an increase in your property taxes.

Kept in its right perspective, owning a home is a great thing. But it is not the crown jewel of your financial plan. For most, it's really just a roof over your head.

I Won't Have "Made It" until I Buy a Home

This is one of the great myths of our culture. People who choose to rent instead of owning a home run into this stigma all the time. When they tell someone they rent, it's treated like a confessional to be discussed in hushed tones. They get a "oh, poor dear" look and the subject quickly changes.

Or they hear:

"It's a good investment to buy a house. As long as you're paying rent, you might as well be building up equity." Or, *"When are you going to settle down? When are you going to take on some real responsibility?"*

Debby is a client in her mid-thirties who rents a home. She has rented all of her adult life, and she prefers it. She is an Executive Director of a charitable foundation. Her co-workers and friends know that she could afford to buy a home, based on her position and the salary she receives.

They keep asking her as a mother would a child, "When are you going to buy a home?" as if there is something wrong with her until she does.

She pays $500 a month to rent a nice house. She would have to pay at least double that to own a home of comparable worth. She is taking the amount she saves each month and investing it in a retirement account. By the time she retires, she will have accumulated a nice nest egg.

We often overlook the benefit of renting in terms of its practical and psychological advantages. Not only is Debby saving money, but she also has the added peace of mind of not having to worry about the care and upkeep of her house. If the basement leaks, someone else has to take care of it.

Another client swears by what he calls "the Zen of renting." He has always found remarkable places to live and never in his life has paid over $500 a month. He values the freedom he feels in being able to move somewhere else if he chooses to, or the freedom to travel for an extended period of time. He does not like to work on things around the house. He doesn't enjoy building, gardening, remodeling, or fixing things. It's someone else's worry.

From a strictly financial view, it sometimes makes *more* sense to rent than to buy. And countless case studies prove it. When you add in the buying and selling costs, the additional mortgage costs, the real estate taxes, and the costs of upkeep, the fact is that *by renting you often come out ahead financially*. Factoring in the tax advantages of ownership does not always tip the balance in favor of home owner-ship.

When you buy a home other costs come "out of the woodwork." That wallpaper in the kitchen just won't do. And those curtains in the living room—they look like they came from grandma's house. Don't you think a deck over the back yard would be nice? And we should replace the plumbing.

When you rent, such expenses don't enter your mind or exit your pocketbook.

If you decide to buy a home, make sure that your decision is not based on peer pressure like *"I am not a respected member of society until I own a home."*

I know a young professional couple who recently moved to Seattle and are renting a home. They have plenty of disposable income and would have no problem qualifying to buy a home. Yet they could not tell me with any conviction that they planned to stay in this area for more than three years. They have parents back east and they wanted to be able to respond quickly if their parents' health failed. They didn't want to be stuck with a house.

They are prime candidates to continue as renters. They should not buy.

Now, let me turn the tables on you. Based on an analysis of your situation, even if renting *does* make more sense financially, it still might be best for you to buy a home, once you factor in the emotional issues.

There are risks involved in renting. You are subject to the whim of the landlord. You may have to move with only a few months' notice. The rent may go up. (However, home ownership does not make you immune to rising costs. Real estate taxes, insurance, and maintenance costs all are subject to rise beyond your control.)

However, you may need the peace of mind brought by the long-term security and stability of owning a house. You may want to have a home you can upgrade or remodel. You might want to develop an extensive garden or make improvements to the landscape. You might want to paint it pink.

Kym Beldon is a client who is an account executive at a media firm. She is also an artist, and she wants to develop a business painting portraits. Her husband is a freelance writer who survives economically by writing copy for commercial clients. He, in turn, would rather work on his own short stories and leave the commercial work behind. The Beldons currently rent a home.

They are thinking of buying a house. Based on their current income level, they can afford one that costs about $170,000.

I said to them, "Are you sure you want to do this? You'll most likely have to keep working full-time at the media company and your husband is going to have to continue doing corporate work for some time to afford it."

Kym said, "We just don't like being at the mercy of the

landlord. We never know when rent is going to go up and we might have to move before we are ready. A house that is our own will give us a base camp that we can rely on. We can then make some long-term planning decisions in our life. And fixing it up will be a form of self expression for us."

Because the Beldons' rent is low, it would allow them the chance to make some career changes they both want. But the need for a long-term base, for the security of knowing that they will not have to move at the whim of a landlord, wins out. It wins out even if it means they will have to continue doing work they do not entirely enjoy. That is okay because it is a lifestyle choice they are making consciously. Another couple in the same situation might prefer to do their hearts' work, even if it meant they'd earn less and have to rent.

To rent or to buy comes down to a lifestyle choice. First look at the facts: What are the true costs of buying versus what does it cost to rent? Once you can clearly see the facts, does it make financial sense to buy or rent? If rent comes out on top, then stand back and ask yourself, "But, do I *want* to rent?" The answer may very well be "no." If so, the emotional issues may outweigh the financial ones.

I tell my clients that most financial planning decisions are based 80% on facts and 20% on emotions—except when the decision is based 100% on emotions. The decision to rent or buy a home is a perfect example of this principle. No matter what the facts are, sometimes our emotions are the real reason we decide to do things. If you run the numbers, they may show that it is more cost effective to rent: the fact. But you may just feel better knowing that the roof over your head is one that you are going to own one day: the emotion. If you decide to buy when the facts suggest differently, that is a decision 100% based on emotion. That's fine, as long as you decide it consciously.

The important thing is to make the decision based on the lifestyle elements that are really important to you. Avoid making an automatic decision to buy because you have been told it's a great investment or because you feel it's necessary in order to be considered a grown-up.

If your reason for buying a home is based on financial issues alone and the analysis shows rent is better, then rent. If you need the emotional security of owning, then buy.

Financially, you'll make few purchases in your lifetime that rival the cost of a home. Study your alternatives closely. Understand your options, and then weigh the facts against your underlying values and emotional needs.

You do not have to buy a home to "have it made." It is equally okay to rent. The choice is up to you.

I Should Pay Off My Mortgage Early

Oftentimes people say, "I really want to pay off my house." I ask them what their mortgage interest rate is. These days, the answer is usually in the 7 to 8% range.

I show them an investment return analysis covering the last 90 years. From 1900 to 1990 (even lopping off the recent years of this exorbitant bull market) a nicely diversified portfolio of 60% stocks and 40% bonds would have earned a 7 3/4% rate of return. And a portfolio allocated 60/40 stocks to bonds is rather conservative. A higher allocation of stocks would have earned a higher rate of return. And as anybody knows, over the last ten years, we have earned returns from stocks and bonds much greater than 7 3/4%.

To pay off a mortgage requires coming up with a healthy chunk of money all at once, or making larger mortgage payments than required each month. Instead of using that money to pay off their mortgage, I suggest to my clients that they invest it. If past history holds true, they will probably earn a return at least equal to their mortgage rate. Even if they earn the same percentage as they are paying in interest, they will come out ahead by keeping their mortgage because they receive a tax deduction for the interest paid on the mortgage.

If instead of applying $100 a month toward early payoff of your mortgage, you took that same $100 and invested it for thirty years at 8%, it would grow to $140,855. If during that same 30 years you made your regular house payments, you would then own your house free and clear, and have a pretty good investment account to boot.

Yet some people will read the simple analysis above and start to sweat. All their life they have had this goal of paying off their mortgage early. Even though, from a rational economic standpoint, they would earn more in the long-run by investing the money in stocks and bonds, they feel better paying off their mortgage instead.

And to them I say: *Pay off your mortgage.*

Every financial decision involves a blend of analytical and emotional factors. We are told that emotion doesn't belong in business or in financial decisions. But, in fact our decisions are often primarily based in them. To deny our emotional needs in financial decisions is to deny ourselves—the part of us that needs to feel good about what we are doing and to feel safe.

Remember that financial planning is usually based 80% on

fact and 20% on emotion—except when the decision is based 100% on emotions.

I often work with couples where one spouse is very analytical. The man arrives with all the mortgage amortization schedules and has all the proof to show his spouse why they shouldn't pay off their mortgage. He listens to me reinforce his position and smiles.

Then I tell them that emotional factors should sometimes take precedence over analytical results and the other spouse lights up. If one spouse has strong emotional reasons to pay off the home, I may support doing that over what the strict financial analysis might show. The emotional drain of not having the mortgage paid off may actually be more costly than the amount of money they are bypassing by not investing in the market. Some people find that the peace of mind that comes from living in a house that is paid for is priceless.

One client worked for a company that was bought by another company. As a result of the buy-out, his stock options increased in value by thirty or forty percent. His net worth increased to over 5 million dollars. Do he and his wife have enough money? Shouldn't that amount of money give them peace of mind? Not in this case. His wife will not be comfortable until their mortgage is paid off.

But he didn't want to pay off the entire mortgage immediately. In the end, they compromised. They made an agreement that 25% of everything from the old company stock that is sold would be diverted and will go toward paying off the house. The other 75% can be invested in the market. This accomplishes what the wife needs and, at the same time, takes advantage of the higher returns they can make in the market.

Paying off a mortgage early may give you peace of mind. Who cares about a few percentage points one way or another if you sleep better at night? Go ahead and pay off your mortgage. Just be clear why you are doing so.

But if optimizing your long-term financial return is important to you, then begin to see your 7–8% mortgage in a different light. You could take the money you would otherwise be spending to pay your mortgage early and invest it in a diversified portfolio that could potentially earn you a higher rate than 7–8% over a time period of ten years or longer. In the long run, you would probably come out ahead.

I Must Buy the Very Best for My Child

Do you have any idea what it costs to raise a child? Are you sitting down? According to a 1998 *US News and World Report* article, a middle-class couple will spend a total of $301,183 on a child born today and raised to age eighteen. Add in four years of college expenses and the total is $459,014 (assuming you will send your child to an in-state public university.) More affluent parents, those making over $59,700 a year, will spend $437,869 to raise a child to age eighteen. If they send the child to a state university, the total reaches nearly $600,000.

For a middle class family, this adds up to $1,395 a month per child, *excluding* the cost of college. For a more affluent family, the cost is $2,027 a month per child.

These costs include pre-natal care, delivery, childcare, housing, transportation, health care, clothing, primary and secondary education, toys, and miscellaneous expenses.

They do not include the cost of lost wages or income as a result of having a child.

Having or not having children is a personal choice that defies a purely economic analysis. However, having embarked on the path of having a child, you would do well to understand the economic implications of the decision.

My clients have a pervasive attitude that their children deserve the very best. They rarely look at the day-to-day cost associated with this attitude—which can be staggering.

Underneath the belief system of having to give their children the very best is a theme mentioned earlier in this book about paying for college: *I cannot deny my kids anything—otherwise I am a bad parent.*

Baby boomers believe they need to give their kids everything, and everything needs to be brand spanking new.

My daughter Angie turned two recently. Her best friend owns one of those little plastic cars that the kids can get in and propel around. Whenever Angie went to visit this friend she climbed in the car and wouldn't get out. She just loved it. So for her birthday, the obvious choice was her own little car. I was about to head out the door to Toys 'Я' Us to buy a new one, when my partner, Chris, told me that one of our mutual friends had an old car their child had outgrown.

"Maybe they would be willing to part with it," Chris said.

"Great idea," I said.

But we couldn't get in touch with them. And Angie's birthday was approaching fast. I said, "I'm just going to buy a new one." I didn't really want her to have a crummy used car anyway. A new one would be better. After all, Angie is my daughter—she should have the best.

"No," Chris said. "Let's keep trying."

The next day we were able to get the used one from our friend. It was perfect. Angie loved it. And guess what? Every day since then, it has sat outside in the rain. It wouldn't have taken long for a new one to look just as used as the car we got for Angie.

Because we love our children, we think we have to spend whatever it takes to get them the best. And we don't question this attitude. We also make the association that "best" means the same as "new." It's ridiculous!

This attitude is particularly prevalent among first-time parents, and they become overwhelmed by all the things they need to buy for the baby. As adults they are used to always buying new, quality stuff. They assume that since adults wear things out, that the baby will, too. So they consider used cribs, strollers, toys, and clothes unacceptable. Before you know it, they are down at the Baby Designer Store and the charge card is flashing, buying the $700 crib with built-in changing table, a state-of-the-art stroller, and of course, designer baby clothes!

They forget that in the case of a crib, the baby just lies

around in it—for about two years. She's not going to wear it out, and she doesn't care if it's made of tight-grain antique mahogany. It's just a crib. The clothes she wears will be outgrown in four months. Are they soft? Comfortable? That's all she cares about—not that her new sleeper suit came from Nordstrom's and cost $35.

The fact is, babies don't need all the stuff we feel obligated to get them. And they certainly don't need it all to be new. I know a family who has bestowed hundreds of toys on their young, firstborn child. The only one he cares about is a little red plastic guitar with three strings. He carries it around constantly and has composed his own "songs." He could care less about all the other stuff.

Practically speaking, the things we buy for our kids are used for a short period of time and sometimes not at all. Go look at all the toys your kids have, including the ones that have been around for years. I bet you will find that they look almost new. And even if they don't, they still work fine. And where do these things end up? First you store them in the closet because you can't bear the thought of throwing them away. And later, when the closet overflows, you throw them away or give them to Goodwill.

Think back on your first four or five years of life. How many of your toys do you remember? How about the clothes you wore? Your crib? Was it these things that made you feel happy and loved? Would you have considered it emotionally devastating if your first rocking chair hadn't been brand new? Is your well-being today based on the fact that you always had new clothes?

A newly-pregnant wife and her husband came to see me for financial planning. They were assessing their financial situation and formulating their goals. They listened to my recommendations about not having to buy everything new for their baby, and they took it to heart. They went to all their friends who had young children and collected all of their hand-me-downs—very nice ones, in fact! They saved hundreds of dollars by not buying new. And if they keep this up over the next five to seven years they will save many, many thousands of dollars.

Some people tell me they just couldn't do that. They couldn't call up a friend or co-worker to ask them about used stuff for their kids. They fear they will be looked upon as unsuitable parents who aren't willing to buy the best and the newest for their kid. And they fear that it will tip the cards that they aren't wealthy enough to buy these things new.

If you have something in your attic or basement that you don't need or use, and a friend expresses an interest in it, are you going to look down on them because of it? Of course not! Nor will other people look down on you when you ask them. Most people are happy to part with these things—you are actually doing them a favor by taking it off their hands.

Now, there are certain times when buying new *is* the

way to go. When my neighbor had her kids' pictures taken recently, she wanted the job done by a professional. She wanted them to have new clothes, so she bought them. The decision was a conscious one, based on a specific situation. It was not the automatic response that since it was for her children, it had to be the best, and it had to be new.

The cost of automatic behavior can really add up. A middle class family spends $301,183 on a child up to age eighteen. A more affluent family spends $437,869. The difference, $136,000, is largely attributable to the number of things bought for the child and a zeal to buy everything brand new every time. Just think what a difference $136,000 can make towards your retirement.

Remember that for children the bottom line is the love, acceptance, and attention you give them, not whether you buy them the best.

I Can't Say No to My Kids

One of the most common myths about money crops up in relationship to our children. It goes something like this: *If I deprive my children, I am a bad parent.* The vogue these days is to lavish on our children everything they desire and then more. We don't want to deprive them of anything.

We have forgotten how to say *no.*

Perhaps we fear losing their love and devotion. Today's families have less time to spend with their children. In more families these days both parents work, often spending extended hours on the job, and more families are headed by single parents. So to compensate for not having as much time to spend with our children, we give them *things,* believing it will make them happy or will demonstrate how much we love them.

Whatever the reason, the situation has grown to absurd proportions. Our kids tell us that they just have to have those $155 Nikes! All their friends are getting them! If we say no, how are they going to look to their friends? We don't want them to feel embarrassed or deprived. We get them the shoes because everyone else is doing it for their kids.

We talk about it with the other parents. We comment on how silly it is and how expensive the shoes are. But we still buy them. We have forgotten how to say no.

If we don't say no sometimes—in fact, if we don't say it *fairly often,* our kids are not going to understand that they can't have everything they want in life. What message do we want our children to learn? That everything they want will be given to them? Or do we want them to realize that there are some limits to what is available—and they can help to earn it, if it's really important to them?

What about a joint effort? "I'll buy you the $50 tennis shoes, but if you want the $155 Nikes, you have to work to make up the difference." By using this approach, you would be teaching them that it's okay to have lofty goals, but you have to work to achieve them.

Walt Poca is 44. His parents provided for him abundantly his whole life, including paying for his room, board and tuition for four years of college. But the thing he remembers most occurred when he was 9 years old. More than anything else, he wanted a red ten-speed Schwinn bicycle. No other kid on the block had a ten-speed yet. His dad, instead of just buying it for him or giving it to him for

Christmas said, "I'll tell you what. I'll pay for half of it, but you have to earn the other half on your own."

Walt took a newspaper route. He sold cookies door to door. In four months, he was delivering papers on his new red ten-speed Schwinn.

"It really made an impression on me," he said. "I liked it, having to earn the money. It bothered me at first. I thought it was unfair. It seemed impossible that I could earn $60 on my own. But I did it. And I have never been prouder. I took care of that bike, too. Something in me really wanted more of that—having to earn my way, at least part of the way."

Walt, like a lot of kids, wanted to be responsible. He enjoyed the powerful feeling of "I did it. I earned that!" He did what it took to get there. It wasn't just given to him. He felt the enormous satisfaction that comes from achieving a goal.

My daughter Marie wanted an American Girl doll. There are six different dolls in the American Girl Doll catalog, and I told her she could have one of them. I made it clear I was not going to get her the entire set and never would. She spent hours deciding which one of the dolls she wanted the most. She loves that doll to this day and takes care of it. She doesn't haggle with me to get her the other ones because I made the limit clear to her. If she wants another one, she can save up her own money.

You don't have to buy your child the entire "American

Girl" catalog just because she asks or begs for it. I know a couple who has given their girls every doll and many of the accessories. They've spent over $2,000, and most of the time, these dolls and accessories are now scattered around their room, neglected and gathering dust.

Kids need and love boundaries. When kids are given everything they ask for during their developmental years, it makes a strong imprint. They grow up believing they *should* have everything. It creates and reinforces a mindset that says the way to get something is to demand it—or always expect that it will be given to you. It eliminates the cause-and-effect relationship between productive effort and reward. It sets in motion a materialistic pattern that will cost both you and your children tens of thousands of dollars over the years.

Steve Arnold is what's called a "trust baby." A trust had been set up for him before he had even learned to walk. All his life, he got everything he wanted without having to think about the cost. All the money he ever needed has always been there for him. He went to elite private schools, got a brand new Jaguar when he was 16, and attended an Ivy League college that was completely paid for.

When he was twenty-one, the trust funds became available to him without restriction. He had hundreds of thousands of dollars, so he didn't have to work.

Unfortunately, he spent all of his trust money. He's fifty-three now and is making a living as a house painter earning $12.50 an hour. It is the only work he can find to support himself. Physically, he will not be able to do this work much longer. He has nothing to fall back on, no retirement, no emergency funds. He is living a subsistence lifestyle.

Without ever knowing boundaries in his life, without ever being denied what he wanted, Steve was unprepared for reality—having to make his own way and living within his means.

By giving your children everything they desire, failing to set clear boundaries, and refusing to say no, you are likely to make your children more dependent on you and others. They will be less apt to solve their own problems, earn their own rewards, and grow up. When the inevitable day comes that they get in trouble, they will likely turn to you, expecting the helping hand that has been there all their lives.

As an adult, Walt Poca was never very adept at managing money. Except for the red Schwinn bicycle, everything else in his life had been given to him. Ironically, he became an accountant, but found himself in constant debt. He eventually left the formal business world to take up a career in filmmaking and theater. It was during this time that his dad won the Washington State Lottery.

Try as he might, Walt could not shake the belief that if he got in trouble, his dad would bail him out. He even felt resentful when his dad began to refuse his requests for support. This dependency was so deeply ingrained that it took him well into his late thirties to let it go.

Make the boundaries clear to your kids. Tell them, "I can afford to get you this pair of roller blades. If you want that other more expensive pair, then you'll have to help make it happen."

Allow your children to participate in the choices about how to spend money and the reasons behind them. Let them know what it costs to run a household.

Tell them, "Okay, you want new Air Jordans. You want a guitar. You want every new game under the stars. You want a clubhouse in the back yard. Here's how much money is available. You decide which of these things you want most. Or maybe you want to save this money and go to Disneyland next spring. You decide. It's your choice. But you can't have it all—unless you want to earn the money to pay for it."

Going through this process will teach your children important lessons they would not learn if everything were just given to them. We don't include our children in financial discussions because we don't want them to worry about money, but including them makes them feel more valued and respected. Don't you sometimes harp on your kids to be more responsible? Involve them in family financial planning, and observe the result!

At what age can you start such a process? When can you reasonably bring a child into the decision-making process regarding family finances and choices? I suggest somewhere around age six or seven. This is when they start comparing what they have to what their friends have. At this stage, the asking for everything to "keep up with the Joneses" sets in.

If you involve your kids in financial planning, you might even be surprised at what they come up with. A friend's daughter thought of starting a silver polishing business. Around the holidays she distributes fliers in the neighborhood and always has plenty of customers.

Have your kids make a list of their goals: going to soccer camp, taking piano lessons, traveling to Mexico. Then have them prioritize which of these are most important, and help them develop a savings plan to achieve some of their goals. You can decide which goals you want to contribute to.

In junior high or high school, let them in on how the family finances work. Let them sit with you while you pay the monthly bills. Let them observe you writing the checks. Or let them write the checks and record them in the register. You can show them how much is left at the end of the month and how much will go for groceries and other needs. This is not intended as a guilt trip, but as an education. It allows them to feel that they are included in the overall picture. And they will have a better understanding of why you sometimes have to say no. As a result of this involvement, they will develop an understanding of good money management that will be invaluable to them later in life.

You certainly don't need to talk to them about 7% mortgage rates and IRA plans. But you can include them in discussions about the financial ramifications of some of the decisions you make. Kids are able to understand and handle a lot more than we give them credit for.

Saying no does not mean you love your children any less, that you are depriving them, nor that you have failed somehow. It means that you are establishing clear boundaries.

While on the subject of kids and finances, let's talk about allowances. There's a way to make your children more conscious about money and allow them to discover the power of saving. It is a method of helping them allocate their allowance.

Tell them that 10% of their allowance has to be given to someone in need. This is the "tithe" allocation. My seven-year-old daughter Marie told me her decision, "I want to give this to poor people who don't have enough food." She puts the money in the food bank jar herself.

Thirty percent of their allowance can be spent on anything they want right now. This is the "immediate gratification" allocation. If they want to spend 30% on movies or candy or whatever, that's their choice.

They need to save 30% for things that cost more. This is the "delayed gratification" portion. They may want a

Nintendo game, an archery set, a camera, or in-line skates. They have to save until they can buy them.

The last 30% is for long term goals, like college, or a trip to South America when they are sixteen.

Each portion of the allowance has its own purpose. Each portion has a lesson that the child will learn from it. Incidentally, the above method of allocation is a valid practice for adults, as well.

For younger kids, give them jars for each portion of their allowance. You won't believe how focused they will become, how fascinated and proud they will be, seeing the longer-term jars fill up. Visitors to your home will be escorted to their room to see their jars of money.

In later years, set up a savings account for the delayed or longer term goals, and they will learn about the power of compounding interest.

I started Marie on a 25-cent allowance. When her long-term jar got full, we set up her savings account at the bank. When her first statement arrived showing she had earned 21 cents interest, her eyes got as big as quarters.

"How did that happen?" she wanted to know.

"Isn't it amazing?" I asked. "All this time while you have been sleeping and eating and playing, your money has been just sitting there growing. And they gave you almost a whole quarter for it."

She couldn't believe it. Now every month, she can't wait until the bank statement comes. She wants to see how much she earned while she was sleeping, eating, and playing.

We all want to be good parents. One way to be good parents is to say no to our children when it's appropriate. We don't have to give in to pressure. We have children who are inundated by marketing, selling, and promotion of products. We live in an era where brand name logos are the "in" things to wear. This influence comes right into our living rooms.

Resist this influence. Saying "no" to it will set your children on a responsible course for the future, and it will make an extraordinary difference to your pocketbook.

My Financial Problems Are the Fault of My Significant Other

Regarding money, I've found that there are four types of people.

The Saver: No matter what, savers have to save money, and they can never save enough. They might agree to save a certain amount, but once they accomplish it they will constantly raise the bar saying, "But I really need to save more." They have to be saving all the time, no matter how much they have already saved.

The Spender: Spenders need to spend in order to keep from feeling too confined. If they aren't spending, they aren't happy. The amount doesn't have to be a lot. It can be $5 here and $10 there. They need to have the security of taking money out of their purse or their wallet whenever they want and buying something. They never go too long without telling you of their need to buy something new—whether for the house, the children, or some hobby. And to them, it's completely justified; they just can't get along without it.

The Worrier: These people are always worried that there isn't enough. If they do have enough to cover their needs, they are afraid that it will go away. They are anxious that a disaster is going to happen. They are concerned that they or their spouse will lose their jobs. No matter what, they wake up in the middle of the night worried about money.

The Avoider: The last thing these people want to do is to deal with or talk about money. They would rather clean out the kitty litter box or the garage than balance their checkbook. They pay their bills late. They file extensions on their tax returns or show up at the post office at midnight to get it filed. They might be in trouble with collection agencies, even though they have money in their checking account. They are uncomfortable about money and will go to great lengths to avoid dealing with it.

Most of us interact with money automatically, based on one of these forms of behavior. We have a certain style, defined by our "type," that colors the way we relate to money. It is this style, the automatic behavior that runs the show. It's what we are prone to do without thinking. A saver doesn't wake up and say, "I'm going to save." A saver just saves. A spender's default behavior is simply to spend.

When couples begin to evaluate their money situation and express frustration at the state of things, one thing often comes to the surface. They believe that their financial problems are the fault of their spouse or partner.

"If he just wouldn't spend so much."

"I can't get her to talk about money."

"She can't say no to the kids. We're always buying new things for them"

"Everything we make he puts into savings and always tells me we don't have enough."

"He spends all this money on basketball games and his racing boats!"

"I'm worried about her losing her job. There is so much pressure on me to provide."

The saying "opposites attract" often applies to finances. Rarely do you find that people in a relationship approach money in the same way. No wonder each thinks it's the other person's fault.

I know a couple who was in constant conflict over money. He was a manager in a large shipping company and made lots of money, but it was never enough for his wife. She had savings accounts and investment accounts, as well as college accounts set up for each of their four kids. They owed little debt and their mortgage was nearly paid off.

The husband felt like he was on a chain. When he wanted to buy something, a great commotion always ensued. She told him it should go into savings. When he did spend money, he did so fearing his wife's inevitable reaction.

When they came to see me, she immediately began blaming him for being a compulsive spender. She did not trust him to oversee the money, because she was convinced it would be squandered away. He blamed her for being obsessive about money. She was too tight and made their lives miserable; he could never have any fun and felt like he was in jail.

"Wait a minute," I said. "Cheryl, you need to save, that's a fact. Nothing is going to change that. Every month, you need to see your savings increase. Norm, you need to have money every month that is your *own* to spend. An amount that is agreed upon and is guaranteed—and you are accountable to no one about it."

I asked them if such a structure were set up to give both of them what they needed, would they give it a try?

They agreed—and it worked. They laugh about it now. Rather than existing in a constant state of irritation or resentment, or avoiding each other for fear of confrontation, he is now learning to say, "Oh, that's what she needs in order to feel safe. She has to save." And she realizes, "That's what he needs to do in order to feel a sense of autonomy and enjoyment. He needs to spend."

They now operate under an agreed-upon plan that specifies how much savings will be set aside each month and how much he gets to spend on his own. He gets his own bank account for this use. In fact, the amount he gets to spend each month increases as certain savings thresholds are met!

If you are in a relationship and the financial situation is frustrating, it's not the other person's fault. It's not the spenders' fault that they need to spend. You have your way of looking at money, and they have their way. What couples need is an agreed-upon plan and structure to accommodate both partners' automatic behaviors, their own idiosyncrasies. And you need to accept the fact that *you cannot change each other.*

On an Internet chat line, one man asked, "How do I make my wife responsible? She spends too much. I am worried about it. How can I get her to see what it does to our finances?"

I told him he couldn't *make* her do anything. I told him to quit trying to change her because it wasn't going to work.

He came back vehemently. He was livid. "She has to change! She has to grow up. How can you call yourself an expert in financial planning and condone such irresponsibility? She must change."

I run into this all the time. Marital problems occur around money when we try to change the other person instead of setting up a *structure* that will meet the needs of both partners. This man's wife is obviously a spender and she needs a structure to allow her to spend while not putting them in the poor house. But this fact is not what he wanted to hear.

The first step is to determine and recognize what type of money person you are. The second step is to recognize what type of money person your partner is, so you'll know who you are dealing with. If you are an avoider and your partner is a saver, you probably will have noticed a savings account that is getting bigger and bigger and bigger. So you say, "Honey, what is your problem? We have all of this savings! Why do we need so much?" And she says, "I don't care. We need more." Your next thought may be something like, "This conversation is hopeless. Her response will always be the same."

But if you recognize and legitimize her needs, then the situation will be far more manageable, and your relationship just might improve accordingly.

The saver needs to recognize that the avoider is never going to eagerly sit down and balance the checkbook. The avoider is never going to take a look at how much is being spent here versus there without prompting. He is not going to be very reliable in terms of paying the monthly bills. The saver should recognize the avoider's value in doing other things in their relationship, and discard the expectation that he will ever be a whiz in financial management.

Recognition and acceptance of each other will remove entire layers of conflict over money.

Some combinations are more troublesome than others. Take an avoider and a worrier. The avoider is going to avoid and the worrier will worry about everything no matter what, and probably nothing productive will get done. Such a combination needs help. They need a bookkeeper or a financial planner or an accountant to help handle their money affairs. Two avoiders may also need the help of someone—otherwise big trouble may lie ahead.

I was talking recently to an executive from the East Coast, an avoider. She said, "I never balance my checkbook and never will. At the office people give me balance sheets and I say, 'What the heck are these? What is this stuff? What's the bottom line?' I tell my accountant to pay my bills. He tells me I don't have enough money to pay the bills. I tell him to find it!"

"What would you do with somebody like me?" She asked.

"I would tell you to do exactly what you are doing," I responded. "Let someone else handle it."

She said, "You mean I never have to balance my checkbook?"

"Never," I said, "Don't even touch it."

"Oh, I like you!" she says.

So don't try and change yourself either. If you are a spender, you will remain a spender. You can, however, get more conscious about it and set up a structure that will give you some measure of control over your spending.

Ray and Jene were a couple who came to me for counseling. He was an attorney and she was a dental hygienist. They made plenty of money as a couple, but they were always fighting over it. They had what I consider to be a pretty typical relationship: He made most of the money and claimed she spent most of it.

It became apparent that Ray and Jene both were spenders. They both spent money on whatever they wanted.

As a team, these two people were spending more money than they were making. When they recognized their habits and developed a structure together, they agreed to give it a try. Within a few months, they had stopped spending more than their income.

It's not the other person's fault. The other person is who they are. You might wish for your partner to change over time, to see things your way. But I wouldn't plan on it.

Recognize how both you and your partner relate to money automatically. Then figure out what kind of structure you might create to support your needs and your partner's needs at the same time. If she needs to spend every month to feel right in the world, agree on an amount. If you are an avoider, agree to talk once a month about money. If you are both worriers, go see a financial counselor and have them help you set up a long-term financial plan.

No matter what type of "money person" you or your partner is, you can find a structure that works for both of you. And when you set up such a structure, blaming your significant other for your financial problems will become a distant memory.

I Don't Have to Worry About Money Issues—My Partner Takes Care of That

In most relationships there is a partner who controls the financial matters. This person pays the bills, keeps the financial records, and may even oversee the family investments.

In many cases this situation is both natural and productive. The more analytical or detail-oriented person normally *should* be in charge of cash flow and record keeping. Some people have a knack for these things.

The less financially-oriented partner can certainly be a man, but more often than not it's a woman. Some women have ideas with respect to money that are false and worth dispelling:

- I'll marry Prince Charming and live happily ever after.
- Women are not capable of understanding financial issues.

- I'm not good at math, so finances are too complicated for me.
- He makes the most money, so it's none of my business.

However, since 95% of women will at some point in their lives be responsible for their finances, either by divorce or death, they need to communicate with their partners.

Problems often arise when couples fail to communicate. The person who pays the bills and who is responsible for cash flow in the household may begin to feel like the yoke of financial responsibility is always on his shoulders. If a problem arises, if money gets short, or if some necessity can't be afforded, then this partner feels he has to solve the problem alone. He doesn't normally look to his spouse as someone who can help. He often sees his mate as inept when it comes to managing money, so he bears the burden all by himself.

The financially-oriented partner can also get hooked into a parent-child relationship with his spouse. The person who pays the bills all the time knows what the family can and cannot afford. The other partner doesn't understand the financial situation and so continues to ask for things. *Can we go on this vacation? Can we buy this new couch? Can we go out to dinner?* The financially-oriented spouse is frequently cast in the role of having to say *no*. He can end up feeling like the "bad guy," the parent. The other person may feel like a child being deprived.

Most often, these roles are not discussed openly. The respective partners just fall into their roles and life goes on. This may or may not work, given the particular relationship. However, the lack of open communication can have serious consequences for the financially-passive partner if she suddenly finds herself alone—as in the case of death or divorce. She is left with all the financial responsibilities, and not a clue as to how to handle them. This partner may not know what insurance policies are in effect, or how to provide direction to a stockbroker, or what bills need to be paid. It is difficult enough to deal with the loss of a loved one. The last thing a widowed or divorced person needs is to have to figure out all the finances, too.

One solution is to have an outside person ready to step in and help the financially naïve partner through.

Some of my clients have arranged for me to step in and assist if such a situation occurs. Cheryl and Tim Harrington are one such couple. Tim knows everything about the finances and has kept all the records over the years. Financial-decision making does not come naturally to Cheryl, and she knows nothing about their money situation. Tim provides all the family income, while Cheryl is the homemaker and has raised the children. The couple is in their fifties, and Tim has already had one heart attack. They have agreed that if he dies, they want me to step in and assist Cheryl in understanding what to do—and to set up financial structures she can operate within.

Even if you can't see yourself in this position anytime soon, it is advisable to prepare ahead. Set up a third party to step in and help in case the non-money minded partner finds himself or herself alone and in need of help.

Having a monthly discussion about financial matters is another way to mitigate or eliminate this problem prior to separation or death. The financially-oriented partner can say, "Okay, here are the bills I am paying. Here is what is left to pay by the 31st. Here is what we have saved for retirement this month. After paying the bills, we have *this* much left to live on for the balance of the month." He or she might ask the less financially-oriented partner for ideas or suggestions on how to handle their money.

If you are the less financially-oriented financial partner, you might need to tell your spouse that you want to know how the money is handled and where the records are kept. You may need to ask for the information to be explained in a way that you can understand. In some cases, this will be challenging, because you may not like to talk about money. That's why you may have deferred to your spouse in money matters to begin with. But there can be a cost to this reliance later in life.

Money should not be the forbidden subject or the weak link in your relationship. But it will end up being that way if there is a great disparity in roles, combined with a lack of communication. The disparity in financial roles may not change, but the communication certainly can.

If the passive financial partner is included in money decisions, he or she will no longer feel like an uninvolved spectator. He or she will no longer have to play the role of the dependent child when it comes to financial decisions. He or she can gain an understanding of the strain it puts on family finances when he or she constantly asks for money to buy something. The passive financial partner might become inspired to make a real contribution, and share in the financial responsibility.

The key to a successful marriage is communication—especially regarding money. That means having regular discussions about family finances, being willing to ask questions and raise concerns, and offer assistance to the other partner in understanding or in actually managing the finances.

Also, remember that another person may need to see information presented in a slightly different way than you. Brad and Leslie Wall exemplified this point. He was extremely detail-oriented. He had spreadsheets and line items from here to eternity to show her in their money discussions. They frequently ended up frustrated with each other and eventually stopped sharing financial information. She just "left it up to him."

In fact, Leslie did want to know. However, she had a different orientation regarding money. She just needed to know the bottom line. How much was left at the end of the month for discretionary spending? She needed to know in total what money went where.

Both partners need to know—as best as is possible—the key points of the joint financial game plan and structure. A good place to start is a joint monthly review of finances—and then an annual review that deals with goals and the long-term financial plan for you as a family.

Both spouses should know where the financial records are. Both should know the location of the safety deposit boxes, what is in them, and where the keys are kept; both should know what credit cards are being used and how to cancel them, if need be. (This is also true for you if you are single. A relative or trusted friend should know where your financial records are kept and what needs to be taken care of on your behalf.)

I know one couple who trades off the bill paying each month. They also trade off filing the tax return each year. This way, both partners are in a position to feel informed and empowered concerning the family finances. It also gives each a break, as the burden is not always left to one person.

Take a look at how money is handled in your relationship. Are you primarily responsible for money decisions and record keeping, or is your spouse? Is there a wide disparity in responsibility and understanding regarding your personal finances? Don't just accept this disparity as "the way it is." Explore ways that the disparity can be lessened. Find more meaningful ways to include each other in financial matters. In short, communicate more with each other about finances. Make sure each partner is comfortable about what to do financially should he or she be left alone unexpectedly. Consider involving an outside financial planner to step in to activate some prearranged structures to help in a transition.

It is an act of love to make sure you and your partner have a clear understanding about money. Remember to keep the lines of communication open.

When I Buy Expensive Gifts It Shows I Love That Person More

I know a couple who is drowning in debt. The IRS is after them. Their credit cards are perpetually at their limit. They pay nearly $375 a month in interest, all of it on costly short-term debt. I was helping them come to terms with their spending habits by putting together a Personal Spending Plan when the wife told me, "You have to budget money for the holidays."

"Okay. What do you need to spend?" I asked her.

"Well, we need presents for the kids and each other."

"How much will that be?" I asked.

She looked at her husband a moment and said, "$1,500 to $2,000."

This was a couple with three college-age kids. The kids were fine, and they didn't really need anything. In spite of being deeply in debt, this couple felt obligated to buy them expensive gifts. To the wife, it meant spending over $1,500 and charging more on their credit cards to do so.

For her, the holidays were a time to show appreciation for her loved ones by giving expensive gifts. When I asked whether they would consider scaling back or eliminating the expensive gift giving, they said it was out of the question. Their need to spend a lot on gifts was automatic, one that was repeated each year during the holiday season. They'd never even considered an alternative approach to the holidays.

Where do we get the idea that we have to show affection with expensive gifts? As though Aunt Mary is only going to love us if we buy her that $150 bread maker for her birthday!

Whenever I put together a Personal Spending Plan for a client, I break his or her expenses into three categories. *Committed expenses* (such as a home mortgage, utilities, taxes, or car payments) are expenses that have to be paid. *Discretionary expenses* are those expenditures in which we have some measure of choice, such as groceries or new clothing. *Very discretionary expenses* are for things that are not truly necessary.

Oftentimes, expensive gifts fall into this last category.

Now, I'm not talking about the small stuff here. An occasional gift of candy and flowers for your sweetheart isn't going to break the bank, and I'm not promoting an end to giving presents. I'm no scrooge. What I am advocating is the application of reasonable restraint in gift giving—

which has reached runaway proportions in many of today's families.

Just look under the Christmas tree of any baby boomer family and you'll see what I'm talking about. Stacks of presents are bulging out from beneath the tree—or two or three gifts for every night of Hanukkah. This is not cheap stuff we're talking about! It can add up to thousands in a season of unbridled gift acquisition for a family, and tens of thousands over a period of years.

One client comes from a large family, and he could no longer keep up with all of the gift-giving demands in his life. He realized he was giving presents because of an automatic compulsion—just because it was the "thing to do." He realized that he was giving presents not from the joy of giving, but because he felt obligated to do so. So he decided to find a way to show his love for his family better than buying them presents.

Since going cold turkey and stopping the gift giving, he has not experienced any loss of love from his family. In fact, he feels as loved as ever, and he enjoys the holidays more. The fact that he receives fewer presents from his family than he used to is fine with him. He would rather utilize the time he previously spent hunting for and buying gifts to visit with his family. He saves hundreds of dollars every year. And without saying so, he believes his family members are secretly glad to have one less person on their lists they feel they have to buy for.

A few years ago, my mom had to give up gift giving and it nearly killed her. She got to the point where she simply couldn't afford presents for her children, or her grandchildren, or her great-grandchildren. Inflation had caught up with her. She wrote everyone a letter that said she just couldn't afford it anymore.

Not for one instant did anyone in the family, including the small children, question her love for us because we were no longer going to receive presents from her.

Maybe the best gift we can give those we love is our time. After all, how much time do we spend dreaming up an appropriate gift, driving to the store, parking, shopping for it, buying it, wrapping it, and then giving it? What if we gave half that much time to someone by taking a walk in the park with them, or having lunch together?

We live in a hyper-consuming culture. It is assumed that we have to join the frantic rush to buy and give expensive gifts. And these days expensive is the norm—a CD costs $17, a good set of roller blades runs $125.

Here's an alternative approach to holiday gift giving. Write down all the people that you bought gifts for last December. Try to remember what you bought and how much you spent (not an easy task for most people). Take a really hard look at the list. What could you do this year that would really make a difference to that person? What would really touch them? How much do you really have to spend? Could you spend half as much as you did last year—

in a very thoughtful and loving way?

Now look again at your list. What alternatives do you have to buying them expensive gifts? What if you had a dinner party for half the people listed? How about sitting down and writing some of them a personal letter? For the children, how about going a little out of your way to do things *with* them? Where could you take them that would provide as much, if not more, pleasure as the new toys that they typically receive as gifts—and end up neglecting a few days later?

Determine up front exactly how much money you will allocate for the holidays, and then stay within this limit. Most of us don't. We approach the holidays without a plan, and end up spending impulsively. Ever bought a gift you thought was too expensive simply because you were out of time? The cost of this approach can be staggering!

Now let's look at the current fad of extravagant birthday parties for little kids. Profitable companies have sprung up to provide these "essential" services for overly-busy baby boomer parents.

When my daughter Marie was four, she went to a birthday party where the hosts rented ponies for the kids to ride. They also rented costumes for each child to wear. The boys got cowboy outfits, and the girls were dressed up in floozy saloon dresses and feather boas. A photographer was hired to take pictures of all the kids. (We then had the opportunity to buy the pictures, of course!) The hosts probably spent $2,000 on this party, and the birthday boy was four years old.

I was in a beauty salon not too long ago. Sitting there, I couldn't help but notice all these girls about eight or nine years old filling the chairs in the pedicure section, getting their toes embellished. I asked my hairdresser what was going on.

"Oh, it's the latest thing," she said. "It's a birthday party! The host parents buy pedicures and manicures for all the kids who will be attending the party. Then they go out to a fancy restaurant."

What have we come to? Pedicures and manicures for eight- and nine-year-olds?

I am a mom. I know how overpowering the urge is to give great presents and to create great experiences for my kids, especially when my kids see their friends getting these things. But is it necessary? Underneath all these superficial temptations, what Angie and Marie really want from me is love, affection, and companionship. The other things, the presents, don't really matter. Often, they've forgotten them within a week.

Ask yourself if the gift giving or the extravagant party is accomplishing what you really want. Does it tell the recipients that you love them more? Does it result in them loving you more because you got them something expensive?

Again, I want to emphasize that I am not against gift giving. If you just *have* to give your sweetie a pearl necklace or the hottest and latest snowboard, then by all means do so. But do so from a conscious and rational point of view. Don't do it because you feel you must automatically give bigger, more expensive gifts in order to secure and preserve someone's love—or to demonstrate your love for them.

I have a friend whose father is 79 years old. In the past year he has had several health crises, including a heart attack. His 80th birthday was approaching. All his kids were trying to decide what to give him for his birthday, and what kind of big party they could arrange to celebrate it.

He sat his kids down and said, "On my birthday, I want to spend time alone with each of you and your children. And from each of you, I want you to write me a letter telling me what you think of me and our relationship." Their dad had never before expressed such affection. The kids were so touched they could hardly speak.

If you took ten minutes and really told the people in your life how much you love them and what they mean to you, you might find lifelong results far greater than any material gift could bring.

I Have to Fully Fund My Retirement Plan Every Year

When people tell me their financial goals, one of the most frequent and automatic responses I hear is: "I have to fund my retirement, *no matter what*."

Recently, a couple came in with $2,000 in credit card debt. Both Doug and June work, and together they earn a fair amount of money. They fund their 401(k) plans to the limit each year. But somehow, this $2,000 in debt at 18% interest seems to hang around, gnawing at them constantly.

"For heaven's sake," I said, "Pay off the credit cards. Pull back a little on your retirement funding for six months and get that debt paid off."

The thought had never crossed their minds. Doug told me, "My dad always said to me, "'Whatever you do don't you ever . . . *ever* . . . not fund your retirement!'" He saw his dad's long finger pointing at him whenever he thought otherwise. For fifteen years, Doug and June's number one financial priority had been to fund their retirement plan.

Doug is a bright man. He's 43, and is chairman of a local Chamber of Commerce, but has continued to do something that makes no financial sense—maximizing his retirement while carrying a load of costly short-term debt. He is paying 18% in interest on this debt and his 401(k) savings is earning 9%. By curtailing his retirement savings for a *short time* and paying off the debt, he would be ahead even after you take into consideration the tax savings of his 401(k).

Doug had been led to believe that funding his retirement was a sacred rule that was important above all else. He couldn't bring himself to divert even a small amount of retirement funds toward something that was eroding his current quality of life.

Doug was actually relieved to hear that it *was* okay to reduce his retirement savings to pay off the debt. In six months, he paid it off and restored his retirement funding to its full contribution level.

I also believe that if you *only* fund things that you think you *should*, and don't fund the things you are passionate about—then what's the point? Life comes filled with obligations—but enjoyment of life is something we tend to overlook, sometimes until it's too late.

When my clients establish a list of financial goals, they often overlook or under-prioritize the elements that would most contribute to their enjoyment of life. The things they feel they are *supposed* to do are always on the top of the list. The things they *want* to do are on the bottom—if listed at all.

Jeri and Bill Ressler told me that fully funding their retirement was one of their financial goals. "And we want to pay for our kids' college education," Jeri said. "And we want to pay off our home mortgage."

After a brief pause, Bill sheepishly added, ". . . and go to Europe."

Under her breath, Jeri responded, "That'll never happen."

In this short conversation, Jeri and Bill had laid their cards on the table, and I was not about to pass up the opportunity to call their hand.

"What did you say?" I blurted out.

They proceeded to tell me their story. After they had married and the kids were still young, they took off to Europe for three months. They lived in a VW van and traveled through France, Spain, Portugal, and Germany. They had a wonderful, magical, and unforgettable time. They remember the trip as romantic and adventurous—they were together, and they were free. On that trip, they committed to each other that they would come back to Europe when their kids were old enough to enjoy it fully.

For years, they told their kids about this commitment to take them on a European adventure. But it never happened. Something else always got in the way, living expenses continuously increased, and college turned out to be a more expensive proposition than they had thought.

Now their son was turning fifteen, and as any parent who has had a fifteen-year-old knows, their time was running out. Not too many kids older than fifteen want to go on an extended vacation with their parents.

Jeri and Bill were worried that if they didn't go next summer, it would never happen. But they didn't see how it was possible financially.

"Go to Europe!" I said.

"But we can't afford it. We don't have any left-over money. We don't have enough saved."

"How much would it cost?" I asked.

We talked to a travel agent and came up with an estimate of $4,000.

"Okay," I said. "Reduce your 401(k) contribution enough, just this once, so that you can save the $4,000 you need to go to Europe by next summer."

They were stunned. "You're a financial planner! You're telling us *not* to fund our retirement?"

"Absolutely," I said. "In fact, I'm telling you that you *have* to go! The opportunity is right in front of you, right here, right now. If you don't go, you will regret it for the rest of your lives. Do you think you are going to get to retirement and be glad you didn't take the trip you two promised yourselves and your kids? I seriously doubt it. Life's too short. Go!"

They stared at me a moment, glanced at each other and then lit up. You would have thought they had just won the lottery! They were like excited children. Before leaving my office, they had committed to a date for the trip.

The following year, the Resslers came in for their annual review. They wouldn't let the meeting begin without thanking me.

"We have memories of that trip," Jeri said, "that will be with us all our lives. We will never forget the time we had together. It was the highlight of our lives and our kids' lives. Who cares that we didn't put that money toward retirement? So what if we have to postpone retirement for a few months? It won't make that much difference. It won't make as much difference in our lives as taking that trip did."

We need to give consideration to those things that create real meaning in our lives and include them in our plans. If we fail to figure them into our financial plans in a real and tangible way, then life has a way of just slipping by.

Many of my clients believe it is irresponsible to do things that would bring them the most satisfaction. They almost need permission to do things that they deeply yearn to do. Most of the time, their dreams are not only possible, but realizable. Quite often, the key to unlocking the dream is to realize that funding their retirement plan does not *always* have to take precedence.

I want to be very clear on this. I'm not telling you to

stop funding your retirement plan *forever*. I am saying it is okay to take a break from funding your 401(k) plan for *one* year, for *a* special circumstance, like the trip of a lifetime, the elimination of debt that is keeping you awake at night, or the financial donation that allows a child to receive a kidney transplant. These are special needs and events that call to you. It is appropriate and rational to temporarily divert some money from your retirement plan to fulfill these experiences.

A couple in their late twenties were committed to fully funding their 401(k) plans. The wife was pregnant and was planning to take six months off once the baby was born. They were concerned about how they were going to afford her time away from work. I told them not to fund their retirement plan that year.

They asked, "Is that okay?"

"Being home with your baby for the first six months of its life is certainly a special circumstance that warrants relaxing your annual savings goal. It's a good reason to pull back a bit from fully funding your retirement for the year," I told them.

This is not about diverting retirement funds in order to buy *things*. Wanting to buy a new car or a new big-screen TV are not good reasons. It is about life experiences that are precious and valuable and that will be lost if not capitalized on. It is about taking all aspects of your life, including the emotional and heartfelt parts, into account in your financial planning. I am simply telling you to invest in these special experiences when they beckon. If you don't, you may lose the opportunity forever.

Yes, you need to fund your 401(k) plan. Yes, you need to plan for your retirement. But just as importantly, you need to fund your dreams.

In reality, most people aren't saving enough for retirement. I usually encourage my clients to save more—but not to the exclusion of a *once in a lifetime* experience that they are really passionate about.

The important thing is to not let any one element of your financial plan become so overwhelmingly important that you exclude your dreams. If you allow yourself to enjoy these experiences fully, the memories and quality of life they bring can never be taken away from you.

Is there a lifelong dream that you have never allowed yourself to consider because you didn't think you had the money? Is there an opportunity that will be lost forever if you don't do it in the next year or two? If you took $100 a month away from your retirement plan for one year, what would that allow you to do that you never thought was possible?

Maybe you don't have to fully fund your 401(k) *every* year. Maybe you can bring to life the experience that calls to you most deeply. Then, when you finally do retire, you can do so with the memory and the peace of mind that you have invested not only in your retirement, but also in yourself and your loved ones along the way.

I Will Retire at Age Sixty-Five

Most people believe that they will work until age sixty-five and then, like their parents, retire and live a life of leisure. Like Mom and Dad, they will spend their autumn years traveling and playing golf.

Mom and Dad are surviving on nothing more than their pension and Social Security. Combined, these benefits provide them sufficient income to live comfortably in retirement. Only in America! Just a few more years and you, too, will be living this idyllic life.

Fat chance. Today, few companies have pension plans like those our parents had. It is now rare for a company to contribute an amount we can live on when we reach retirement age.

Most companies have shifted the responsibility for retirement funding from them to us. Guaranteed benefit pension plans, where the company provides a set retirement income, have been supplanted by 401(k)-type plans. These plans are dependent on employee, not employer, contributions and they will only provide us retirement funding based on the level of our own contribution, and the performance of the investments in the plan we choose.

We are such a mobile workforce today that, even if we do work for a company that provides a traditional pension, few of us will work there long enough to qualify for much of a benefit. We no longer stay at jobs twenty, thirty, or forty years like our parents did.

And Social Security is not what it used to be. Its original intent was to only take care of life's most basic needs after retirement. An individual today earning $60,000 will find that Social Security funds only 29% of her retirement needs. Assuming she is forty-five years old today, Social Security will provide her a meager $18,226 a year when she finally reaches sixty-five—and that's if Social Security, as we know it today, is around at all.

The government's original goal of providing a financial safety net to the elderly through Social Security is a faded memory. Social Security benefits have diminished to the point where they are now just a meager income supplement. You can't live on Social Security. I have some clients in their twenties and early thirties who don't count on it being there at all by the time they reach retirement age, and I support their approach. When I do retirement calculations for my clients who are fifty or younger, I don't even include Social Security in the equation.

For many people, the belief that their current retirement funding will be sufficient is often based on hope rather than facts.

Leslie Wetzel was a teacher approaching retirement. She told me that when she retired, she would need only $1,600 a month to live. This amount would cover her basic living expenses and the cost of her greatest desire: traveling to various parts of the country each year to visit her grandchildren. She believed that her teacher's retirement benefit, Social Security, and some money she had saved would cover all these needs. She wanted to make sure that she would always have $1,600 a month to spend, given her life expectancy and inflation.

She was retiring at the end of the month. The school district was already planning a party for her. But based on my calculations, the most she could spend was $1,200 a month.

By the end of the session, Leslie was in tears. It was twenty-four days before her retirement, and she had discovered that she would not have enough. As she was walking out the door, she murmured, "Maybe I can go back and ask them if I can work part-time for awhile."

It was probably the saddest session I've ever had with anyone. She had waited too long to find out the bad news.

Leslie's situation came from the typical and automatic

belief that if we work hard for many years, we will be taken care of in retirement. It is based on an old belief that someone is looking out for us, that what we have in our retirement plan and Social Security will be enough.

It probably won't work that way. Of my hundreds of clients, only a small percentage have adequately saved or are making adequate contributions to their retirement. Only those who have lucrative stock options from their company, an inheritance, or have managed to accumulate a sizable portfolio, truly have what they need for retirement.

Most people presume they will save this big nest egg so that they won't have to work anymore in retirement. However, they rarely realize how large this nest egg will have to be. A forty-five-year-old person who currently has $150,000 in a retirement fund, and who wants to live on $4,000 a month from age sixty-five on, will need a portfolio value at retirement of $2,320,000. He or she will need to save $4,200 a month for the next twenty years to amass this amount. (This example assumes a 4.5% inflation rate, an average rate of return of 7.5%, and a life expectancy of ninety years.)

What this means is that in all likelihood, most people will need to work past age sixty-five. Age sixty-five was an arbitrary age to begin with. When Social Security was created in 1935, the average life expectancy was sixty-three. Today, we still hold age sixty-five as the standard retirement date, even though the average life expectancy has increased to eighty-four years.

There is another reason to consider working past age sixty-five. It stems from the myth that at age sixty-five—at last—we will be able to kick back and do what we want. We'll have unlimited time to garden or fish or stay at the beach cottage.

We are forgetting one thing.

That's not what people in our generation are likely to want to do when they retire. We as baby-boomers have been raised in a dynamic, goal, and achievement-oriented world that encourages physical activity, interpersonal contact, and accomplishment. I doubt that we're going to be satisfied just sitting on the porch at the cottage. I suspect that we're going to want to be busy, active, productive, enterprising, adventurous, and eager to find new experiences.

It would be sad to work thirty, forty, or fifty years so that we can retire, then find ourselves there and say, "Is this it? Is this all there is?" It might be great for a while, but I've been told that lounging around gets a little old. I know people who have retired to their condo on the golf course and after a short while tell me, "I can't just play golf everyday. It's not enough for me."

Chances are, you will have twenty, thirty, or maybe even forty years left after retirement.

What if you structured your retirement so that you could stay active, and at the same time keep earning

$10,000 or $15,000, or even $20,000 a year? You could look forward to working part-time, or on a consulting basis.

A good friend of mine is retired and now works at an ice cream shop in a small seaside town. She does this three or four hours a day and earns about $10,000 a year. It keeps her connected and gives her the feeling that she is doing something worthwhile. She enjoys the contact with other people, and she doesn't think of it as work. To her, it's fun.

Many people are working later in life by choice. Many are working part-time. The bottom line is that many people have discovered the need to stay useful, active, and constantly learning. It might be a small business, teaching at the local community college, a stint with the Peace Corps, or serving as a mentor for a younger person.

Steven Grindle is a retired corporate executive who worked for a desktop publishing company. However, his true passion is poetry, and he is currently writing a book of poetry that his wife is illustrating.

He decided that writing could be a vehicle to help troubled teens. He thought it might help some of them resolve difficult issues they have had to deal with in their lives, so he now teaches a creative writing class once a week to kids who are in juvenile detention. He told me that the stuff these kids are being given permission to write is, on one level, very brutal, but on the other hand, very cleansing.

One kid was very quiet during the entire class. As Steven went through a discussion of various writing styles, this kid just looked out of the barred window, bored and distracted.

When it was time to write, he wrote about seeing his parents killed in front of him at age five and how since then, he has never trusted anyone. He knew he had to take care of himself, because no one else would.

Once he started, Steven couldn't get him to stop. The kid wrote and he wrote. For the first time in his life, he consciously re-entered the pain and the anguish of what he had experienced. From that place, he began to heal.

Steven told me that everything he ever did in his corporate life paled in comparison to seeing that one kid begin to turn his life around. Steven is retired, but he has never felt more alive, productive, and useful. Steven has discovered that in many respects, life after age sixty-five can be richer than before—and it doesn't have anything to do with money.

I encourage my clients to begin now to find work they love, regardless of their age. Baby-boomers' parents did not concern themselves a great deal with finding work that they enjoyed. A job was required, and retirement was the reward for working for forty years. I have clients who have this mentality—they work at jobs they don't like and tell me they "just need to hang on until retirement."

They think they'll just follow in their parents' footsteps. They see their parents retire at sixty-five from long, successful careers, and begin a new existence of leisure. But is that going to work for us? It actually doesn't even work very well for many of today's sixty-five-and-over population, either. The search for a deep and fulfilling purpose in life spans all generations, and it does not have to wait until age sixty-five.

A couple in their late fifties both worked, owned a home and two cars, shopped where and when they wanted, and went out on the town whenever they felt the urge. In short, they had a lifestyle characterized by *enjoyment now*. They had saved some money for retirement, but not very much. They both wanted to retire at age sixty-five, and they asked me to do a retirement calculation for them.

I told them I wouldn't do it. It would be a waste of their time and money. The amount they would have to save each month to be able to retire at age sixty-five and sustain their current lifestyle was more than their current disposable income.

I talked to them instead about finding careers that they could enjoy now—and could spend the next twenty to twenty-five years building and developing. I also talked to them about reducing their current lifestyle so they could save more toward retirement.

I asked them what they could do in retirement that might bring in $20,000–25,000 a year. The wife answered immediately, "I'd go to work for a non-profit organization as an administrative support person."

Her husband was shocked. "You've got that figured out

already?" he asked.

"You bet," she said. "You tell me I need to earn $25,000 in retirement. For that, I'd go work at a non-profit organization in an instant—because that's where my heart is."

There was no way she could live on so little now. The couple had financial demands far in excess of what such a job would bring in. But for her, it served to establish a vision of what she would be doing when she retires from her current job. It gave her something she could look forward to. It gave her some time to plan the means for this transition later in life. She could now begin developing the contacts that might make the transition to the non-profit world smoother.

Knowing she has to earn that extra income beyond age sixty-five made her question continuing in her current job until retirement. She began to re-examine her devotion to a job she did not like very much—a job she had programmed herself to keep for the next fifteen years.

The time to take a close look at your retirement plan is *now*. How much are you saving a month, and how will that provide for you when you are in your late seventies and eighties? Are you investing these funds for long-term growth? How much should you reasonably expect to receive from Social Security? If you are like most people, you will find that you will not have enough to completely retire at sixty-five. In the end, you will be able to make withdrawals from your nest egg, but still have to supplement that with additional income from some type of work, at least for a while. Even though this may be bad news to some of you, it's better to hear it now, while you can do something about it, and plan accordingly.

Many people have the opportunity in their current careers to develop skills that they can utilize for consulting part-time after retirement. Of course, this is all the more reason to find a career that you enjoy now.

One client, an accountant, did tax returns for businesses. When he retired, he began consulting for small businesses. He charges $100 an hour and works about twenty hours per week.

Another client worked in human resources for twenty years. She developed skills that allow her to consult part-time for start-up companies, setting up their human resources departments. Her "retirement" is anything but—she has no plans to quit working, because she's having too much fun!

If you're not in a career that you enjoy, start the process of finding one. When you are engaged in work that you love, retirement is no longer such a high priority. For many who follow this path, retirement is no longer their life-long goal! They find happiness is in their work.

On the other hand, if you truly want to opt out of your current line of work at age sixty-five, then do so. Be creative in finding ways to supplement your retirement income with something you enjoy. Be an espresso barista, make jewelry, teach sewing classes.

People put an enormous amount of unnecessary pressure on themselves because they fear they will not have enough money to retire at age sixty-five. I have experienced this forlorn look in my clients so many times. They come to me armed with their *Money Magazine* quick calculation on retirement, and saying, "Oh my God, I won't have enough!"

How can you channel that negative energy and fear into something that works in your favor?

I suggest four things:

- Save as much as you can for retirement—the sooner the better.
- Plan to work past age sixty-five.
- Look for ways to supplement your retirement income once you have retired.
- Begin now to live a simpler, less expensive lifestyle.

Whatever your age, start now to visualize and plan your lifestyle after retirement. Embrace the idea that you will have a longer life expectancy, and that you may be working past age sixty-five. Do the necessary financial calculations (or get someone to do them for you) so that you will know what you can expect when you do retire. And start doing now what you enjoy doing.

Since they chose to start a family later in life and have

taken on all the associated expenses of children, they are realizing that they'll be working longer than imagined.

Sonya and Jack Foster are such a couple. At first, the thought was a little depressing. They really hadn't expected to work as hard as they have been for that many more years, but they did acknowledge that they enjoyed the stimulation and sense of accomplishment. They had to admit that they loved their work and would miss it if they were retired.

I asked, "What else would you do, once you retire and have more time, that you're not currently doing?" Sonya immediately said she would volunteer at their daughter's school. Jack wanted to lift weights twice per week.

But as things stood, they assured me there was no way it could happen. I asked, "What could you change that would free up time in your life right now?" They looked at each other, and simultaneously said not having to drive forty-five minutes each way to their daughter's school.

Since this discussion, they have moved to a house within walking distance of their daughter's school. Sonya volunteers there every Thursday morning, and Jack now lifts weights on Tuesdays and Fridays. Creatively find time to do those things that will add to your life right now. You don't have to wait until "retirement."

"I'm too busy" has become almost a mantra for baby boomers. We work like mad to keep up with our financial responsibilities, and put off things we think we don't have time for. Sometime in the future, we say, we'll have the time for them—maybe after we retire.

You have time now—it's a matter of priorities. Search for work that you enjoy and start doing it. Begin now to build into your lifestyle those things that bring you pleasure and which you can do for the rest of your life. Then, working past age sixty-five won't be as big a deal, because you will have built a richer and more fulfilling life—both personally and professionally—that will go on well past sixty-five.

I Have to Buy the Latest Upgrade

Tom and Didi Case are in their mid-fifties and are planning to retire in ten years. They make regular contributions to their 401(k) plans and receive matching company contributions. Their income has gradually risen to its current level of about $100,000 a year—and their standard of living has risen to keep up with it. They said they couldn't possibly live on less than $5,000 a month when they retire.

Based on their current and projected retirement savings, they would have to work *significantly* longer than age sixty-five to achieve this level of income in retirement, or they could bite the bullet, simplify their lifestyle, and learn to live on less now.

Because people grow accustomed to spending everything they make, they set themselves up for a fall when they retire. Rather than living below their means, they live *up to* (and often beyond) their means. During their working years, they grow accustomed to a standard of living that they cannot afford once they retire.

If we are successful in our careers, we can expect to get regular promotions and pay increases. And invariably, we opt to take advantage of the opportunities these afford. There is a model in economics called the "marginal propensity to consume." Numerous studies have found that when people receive an increase in their income, they don't save it—they spend nearly all of it. Many of my clients are working extremely hard, in stressful conditions, and for long hours. In doing so, they make a handsome income. In fact, they make more than they need, but you'd never know it—they simply *live up* to that income by buying as many new things as they can. A lawyer client of mine calls this "creeping materialism."

Is your life *so* enhanced by that big-screen, surround-sound home theater that you just can't live without it? Well, how is it going to compare to the 19″ model you can afford when you retire, after your big-screen surround-sound home theater goes on the blink?

We set ourselves up so that retirement seems like deprivation. We do so by living a lifestyle we can't maintain. Then, when we get to retirement, we ask, "Why did I slave all those years and burn that midnight oil? For *this*? This puny little TV?"

One approach to retirement is to begin to live more simply now, at the income level you will have in retirement. Better to live a moderate lifestyle both now and in retirement than to live high on the hog now and in deprivation after retirement.

Step back and ask yourself whether you really need the latest and greatest of everything. Was it really necessary to purchase that new sport utility vehicle sitting in your driveway? Perhaps you could have gotten by with a good used one, or invested a little in refurbishing your old wheels. Perhaps in using this approach over a long term, retirement won't be about deprivation. It will be about maintaining the lifestyle you have grown comfortable with and can sustain.

Computers, stereos, adventure sports equipment—we just have to have the latest. A quality new shirt can run $85, a tie, $50. The house just has to be remodeled. And of course, we need all of it brand new. The latest. We are such a consumerist society that we no longer question these things.

You don't need to replace something just because a newfangled one comes along. How many things do you have in your life that you spent good hard earned money on, that are sitting in the attic or in the basement? Consider them the next time you feel the urge to buy something new.

A client just shelled out $42,000—more than half his after-tax income—on a new car. I asked him why he did that. He told me that his old car was four years old and it was time to get a new one. Four years old!

The brain of the average American is pre-programmed to march down to the local car dealer every three to five years, dicker for five minutes on the price of a glossy new set of wheels, and then sign a contract that costs more than a home mortgage did a few short years ago—not to mention depreciation, which averages 25% in the first year.

I'm not against buying a car which represents the fulfillment of a lifelong dream. In fact, I support it. I have clients who have yearned for a particular car for ten, even twenty years. They have wanted that black '66 Mustang fastback or that '53 Corvette convertible since high school. To them I say, "Go ahead. Buy it if you can afford it." To buy something special in fulfillment of a long-term dream is different than buying a new toy just because everyone else does. The naive belief that a new car every few years is necessary costs a lot of money—money that won't be there in retirement.

The calculations for Tom and Didi Case showed that upon retirement, they could afford living expenses of about $4,000 a month. I asked them to investigate how they could reduce their current living expenses of $5,000 a month and begin to live on $4,000 a month now. They could then save the extra $1,000 and apply that toward retirement. They are going through this process. If they are successful, retirement will not result in any substantial change in their lifestyle, and with the extra $1,000 per month of savings, they could have more than $4,000 a month to spend. Retirement may not turn out to be about deprivation for them.

Remember that your retirement will likely last from twenty to forty years. That is a long time to live in a state of deprivation. If you begin to live below your means now, this simplified lifestyle will last for the rest of your life—and the extra money you're putting away will raise your retirement lifestyle.

Is your current spending consistent with your most important values? Does buying those new upgrades really increase your well-being and your happiness? Is your car a status symbol or is it a means of transportation?

I have a client, Matt Rivers, who acquired a great deal of wealth in a business transaction and was able to retire. While working, he had grown accustomed to an upper-class lifestyle—big house, new car, expensive suits. Recently, he purchased a small cabin in the country and is spending more and more time there.

The last time I talked to him, he said, "You know, it's really great out here. It doesn't matter what I wear. It doesn't matter that I don't throw lavish parties. And you know, I need that baby blue Mercedes convertible sitting in my driveway like I need a hole in my head. I love it out here so much I'm going to sell my big house in town. Who needs it? I'll get a small condo downtown and spend most of my time in the country."

Another client, Kate Martin, is a counselor at a local college. She recently bought a lakefront cabin. She is in love with it, and she made extensive plans to remodel the place: upgrade the bathrooms, rebuild the deck, remodel the kitchen. Since she has been working full-time, she has been unable to devote the time it takes to get all these projects done. She was also worried how she was going to pay for it.

She came in last week and said, "You know what? I'm not going to do all those things now. I'm going to wait until I'm not working, and slowly do them one at a time as I can afford them. And it will be cheaper since I'll be able to do a lot of the work myself."

She is learning to live now within her means and has her eye peeled on sustaining this lifestyle in retirement.

Do you really need the latest upgrade? When you go to buy a washing machine and there are twelve models to choose from, do you need the one that tells you the exact temperature of the water, and that has auto-static removal? It's $125 more than the one that just washes your clothes.

Do you have to have the latest VCR—the one that can record, do special effects, and edit sound? Do you really need your TVs to show you three channels simultaneously? Do you really need the satellite dish that gives you 250 channels?

I have a client who, whenever he goes to buy something, asks himself, "Can I live without this?" He is amazed by how often the answer is yes. Then he walks away without looking back.

Potentially, we have a lot more money available to us now than we will have when we retire. We spend nearly all of our income just because it is there. If we get a raise, we spend it—but we don't need to. The key to not feeling deprived at retirement is to begin to live now the lifestyle we can sustain for the rest of our lives—to start spending less than we make.

The next time some hi-tech or expensive thing in your life breaks down, pause and ask yourself if you really need it. Ask yourself if it, or the other things you set out to buy or upgrade, bring you true happiness. Maybe you can live without them.

The happiest older people I know live within their means. So can you. You can start by resisting the automatic "buying and upgrading" urge. Start to develop a lifestyle now that you can afford for the rest of your life.

I Can Plan for Retirement Later

Often, we as people are afraid to plan for retirement, because it forces us to come face-to-face with our future, and we may not be comfortable with what we see. It fosters thoughts of dying, aging, losing vitality, and having to live on a lot less money—perhaps of not having enough. So the easy way to deal with this dilemma is to put it off. We just don't think about it or deal with it. It's the same reason we put off making wills; it forces us to confront the fact that we really are going to die.

Baby boomers, especially, tend to harbor a "live for the day" attitude. "I'm right here, right now, and that's what matters. The future will bring what it brings. Things will work out somehow. Life is here to enjoy."

A major life insurance company conducted a recent survey on retirement funds. They found that only 40% of working people have any type of retirement plan in place.

Of those who have a retirement plan, only 26% believe they are saving enough. Baby boomers, especially, are falling behind.

For people aged eighteen to thirty-two, the average monthly retirement savings increased by 18% in 1997. Those between fifty-two and retirement age boosted their monthly savings 42%. But baby boomers, those in the middle range, saw their average monthly retirement savings fall by 10%!

Despite these facts, the average worker still plans on retiring at age sixty-two. The gap between what people expect from retirement and what they are actually funding continues to grow. A full 67% of those polled expect to have the same standard of living they had during their work years—or better.

If people would only do something about their retirement now instead of later, it would make a tremendous difference. Assuming a 9% return, a person who is twenty-two and saves $2,000 per year for nine years (for a total of $18,000) will see this amount rise to $580,000 by the time he or she is sixty-five. If this same person waits until he or she is thirty-one to begin, he or she will have to save $2,000 a year for thirty-five years (for a total of $70,000) to even accumulate $470,000 by age sixty-five. In other words, that person would have to save $52,000 more in order to end up with $110,000 less.

I love it when my clients in their twenties and thirties

start funding their retirement. The amount they need to save on a monthly basis is so much smaller than my clients who put it off until they are in their fifties.

Many "generation X'ers" have no problem with saving for retirement. I am seeing more and more of them. They say, "I see what's happening to my parents. That is not going to happen to me. I am going to start planning and saving now."

Ron and Jonna work in the publishing industry. They are both in their thirties and are just getting started on their careers. As a couple, they are making about $60,000. They asked me to show them what it would take to retire at age fifty, and also at age sixty-five. They want to know now what they need to be putting away. They don't even think about buying new cars or the latest upgrade. They are focused on their long-term goal of retiring at age fifty. It shapes their entire lifestyle.

They don't feel deprived of anything. They are very satisfied with the lifestyle they lead, and they gain a great deal of peace of mind by having a retirement savings program in place that will accumulate into a substantial amount by the time they retire, potentially at 50.

I'm not knocking "here and now" living. We should enjoy life, but that notion alone is not good retirement planning. Eventually, the future becomes now, and that's when you will wish you had planned for it. Let's face it—starting a savings plan just before retirement doesn't make a lot of practical sense. You can live in the here and now, but you still need to make adequate preparations for the future.

Our parents didn't have to plan for retirement, but we do. We have to get out the map and chart our course.

Sometimes, people without a clear picture of their retirement needs and funding ask me how to begin. The first step is to gather information about how much you are currently spending on a monthly basis. Look at what expenses may go up after you retire and which may go down. This exercise will give you an idea of how much money you will need in retirement to live. Then take a look at what income you can expect, and from which sources: Social Security, your 401(k) plan, your company's pension plan if you have one, etc.

If you are comfortable with spreadsheets and financial calculations, you can use this information to calculate how much you will have at retirement, and how long it will last (be sure to factor in inflation). If you are not conversant with financial calculations or are intimidated by all this, take the above information to a Certified Financial Planner and have him or her do the calculations for you.

No matter what the numbers tell you, you will be glad you took the first step. The numbers will tell you what you need to do, whether it is to increase the amount you are currently contributing, or to reassess your projected retirement age or desired income level. You might even be pleasantly surprised to learn that you are on the right track.

The first step is always the most important. By taking it, you will have stopped putting off retirement planning for later. Regardless of how old you are, sit down and look retirement planning straight in the face. If you've waited a long time, the reality may be jarring—but less so now than it will be next year or the year after. Get started now. No one else will do it for you.

I Have to
Save, Save, Save!

A few years ago, Yvonne and Leon Redhook came to see me. We did a comprehensive financial analysis of their situation. We inventoried their goals, took a look at their insurance policies to see if they were sufficient, evaluated their portfolio, did a retirement projection, and completed a college tuition calculation for their two kids.

Given the ages of their kids, the colleges they had in mind, and how much they had already saved, we determined the Redhooks had to save $250 per month for each child until their kids started college. They committed to that level of savings and religiously banked the money. They also agreed to save an extra $500 a month for their regular investments, and another $375 a month to put into their IRAs.

Last year, they came in to see me, and they were a bit forlorn. "Our income has dropped off," they said. "The company we work for has reduced our benefits package, and as a result, our disposable income has gone down. We are going to have to make some changes. We don't know where we're going to come up with the $500 a month to fund our kids' college."

"Well, let's take a look at it," I said.

We compared how much they had saved to date to the amount needed for their kids' college. Because they had saved religiously and because the return on their investments had been higher than we projected, it turned out that they had already reached their goal. I had assumed they were going to earn 5% after taxes, but they had actually earned 13%. I ran the numbers on three different computer programs, and in each case, the results showed that they had already saved enough.

"I have some good news for you," I said. "You don't need to make any more payments into the kids' college funds."

The Redhooks were ecstatic, to say the least. Instead of saving for years to come, they could stop saving for their kids' college expenses now.

They had been prepared to make significant lifestyle changes to have the $500 per month they had agreed to save for college. They were thinking of selling one of their cars, were prepared to stop eating out at restaurants except on rare and special occasions, and were considering cutting back on their retirement savings.

However, they didn't have to alter their lifestyle even though their income had gone down!

It was the perfect example of the need to review your savings plans regularly. If you set up a savings plan for a specific purpose, you need to revisit it to compare its actual performance to what you planned. Otherwise, you won't know whether or not you are on track.

Many people have no plan at all. They save an arbitrary amount each month, say $500 for college or some other long-range goal, but they fail to base this amount on reality. They know they need to save—but they have no clear idea of how much the actual need is, and therefore don't know whether or not they are on track toward their goal.

To these people especially, an analysis is in order. There is no telling how much sacrifice and deprivation they may have imposed on themselves in order to make their savings goals—goals that may have been reached long ago.

When she was fifty-two, Diane Gladu came in to review her investments. She was working as a buyer for a fashionable department store, and one of her financial goals was to retire in three years. She had worked for the company for thirty years and would qualify for retirement at age fifty-five. She came in hopeful, but I could tell she was worried underneath. I asked if she wanted me to run a retirement calculation for her, but she turned me down. I didn't press it—she had other priorities in her life that were more imminent and that needed attention.

Diane was the classic example of someone who did not want to confront the numbers about retirement because she was afraid of what they would tell her. It took her almost until the eve of her retirement date to come in and say, "Okay, I'm ready to look at the retirement calculation. I hope you tell me I can retire." The results showed that she had more than enough money to allow her to retire. In fact, she had enough to last her until she was 110 years old!

For Diane it wasn't a matter whether she could have retired earlier—she had to work until age fifty-five in order to qualify for her pension. But imagine what her last ten or fifteen years would have been like if she had known that she was going to have plenty of money in retirement. She could have used some of the money she had been saving for retirement for other goals in her life!

Consider the psychological peace of mind she would have gained had she evaluated her retirement plan earlier. For the last ten or fifteen years, she had lived in constant worry that she wouldn't have enough even though she had plenty—and then some!

Your savings plan might be for college or for retirement. It might be for a down payment on a home, the purchase of a new car, or an exotic vacation. By checking your savings plan periodically, you may discover that your rate of return has been higher than you projected. If you are reaching your goal faster than originally anticipated, you can make a downward adjustment in your monthly savings and have money available for other goals.

Every year, take a look at your goals, whether they are college funding or saving for a down payment on a country home. Look at how much you have saved to date. Based on the rate of return you have received and you expect to receive for the ensuing years, you can project how much you will have in the future. Determine how close you are to achieving your goal.

You may discover that you no longer have to lie awake at night worrying, or that you can do some of the things you never thought you would be able to. You may find inside your savings plan for college or for retirement that you have a cruise to the Caribbean waiting for you—right now.

It Is Selfish to Spend Money on Myself

Some people harbor a deeply-ingrained belief that it is not okay to spend money on themselves. They won't hire a baby-sitter or a house cleaner to give them a much-needed and well-deserved break. They wouldn't think of indulging in a massage or surrendering to the need for a counseling session, and they rarely treat themselves to a concert or a movie. These are people that go for two years without new clothes.

These same people give their kids everything, but they deny themselves the simple pleasures of life.

Where did this idea come from that it is not okay to spend on ourselves? Why do some people single themselves out for a life of deprivation?

The idea of sacrificing oneself for the good of the family often shows up in the person that does the budgeting. The person charged with the task of trying to balance the family finances has a sense of duty and responsibility that can sometimes lead to self-denial.

The problem with "everybody else is first" is that over time, it can lead to a feeling of resentment. Beneath the surface, some reward is expected in return for all this giving—but it seldom or never comes. The person making the "sacrifice" may gradually become unhappy, because he or she is not attending to his or her own deepest personal needs.

People who respect themselves and treat themselves well have much more to give, while a person who continually denies himself or herself eventually runs out of steam.

People often use money as the excuse for not taking care of themselves. "We just can't afford it. I have to get the kids ready for the new school year. We're just not getting ahead—I'll make these shoes last another year." However, the true issue is often not money, but an unwillingness to replenish oneself.

The most successful caretakers are those who do not deny their own needs, and *everyone* has needs. Maybe it's a massage or a facial, a new CD, a weekend camping trip with the guys, or a new leather coat. These are the little things that reward our efforts and restore us.

It is not selfish to take care of yourself. It is a great investment. You may feel you can't afford that weekly massage; however, if the result is that it makes you feel centered, gives you peace of mind, eliminates your resentment toward work or home life, and restores your energy and happiness, then perhaps you can't afford *not* to do it.

One client continually denies herself for her children or her husband. She attends to their needs constantly and expends great effort to make their lives easy, convenient, and trouble-free. She buys them everything they need and everything she *imagines* they need. On top of this, she works in a highly demanding profession.

She told me, "I don't know if I am Cindy the Mom, Cindy the Wife, or Cindy the manager. Who is Cindy? That's what I want to know."

I said, "If you want to discover Cindy, then do something nice for yourself. Take a walk every day and smell the roses. Go for a weekend by yourself somewhere."

There is an adage that you have to give to receive. But, did we leave ourselves out in the process? Maybe it means that we also need to give to ourselves in order to receive the strength and stamina and energy to give to others. If we don't invest in ourselves from time to time, then we will have less to give to others. We need to recharge our batteries.

Larry and Colleen Wilder have a daughter in high school. Although they are not wealthy, they make a good income. They came to see me to put together a Personal Spending Plan.

Colleen is a very dutiful parent, attending to her daughter with the utmost of care. She concerns herself with her husband's well-being, and she is always doing things for other people.

She also has her own passion—Colleen is fanatical about raising and training border collies. She travels with them in order to let them do what they love to do—herd sheep into corrals. Whenever the subject turns to border collies, she has the enthusiasm of a girl with a new doll, and she can talk for hours about them.

However, she was always apologizing to her husband about the money she was spending on vet bills, dog food, training classes, and equipment. When she wanted to breed a dog, it cost money. As her number of dogs increased, it became necessary to add to her flock of sheep so there would be enough to herd. Competitions cost money to enter, as did the barn and the feed. There were never-ending expenses that came with her passion, and she was always apologizing for how much she was spending.

She didn't feel she could just go spend that money on her passion. She felt like she needed to apologize for it.

The fact was that her husband and her daughter completely and enthusiastically supported her. But she wouldn't allow herself to acknowledge that fact. She believed that it wasn't okay to spend money on herself.

We put together a spending plan that included all the

necessary expenses for the family, the retirement savings, college savings, and other long-term goals. When we got to the line item concerning raising her collies, Colleen began a litany of excuses and apologies.

"Wait a minute," I said. "Let's first find out how much this really costs."

When we added it up, and she saw the actual figure, she was surprised. "Well, we can certainly afford that," she allowed. For the first time, she stopped trying to justify it.

I said to her husband, "Is it okay with you for Colleen to spend $175 a month on the dogs?"

"Absolutely!" he said. "She's so alive when she's training her dogs. She is a joy to be around. Our daughter is so proud of her that she brags to all of her friends. Of course we want her to spend that money! It adds so much richness to her life!"

Awestruck, Colleen looked at him and said, "Really? You really mean that?"

"Of course I do," Larry said. "I've told you that before. It's okay. In fact, I don't want to live with you if you don't do the things you love. It's okay, honey. Go for it!"

Colleen was speechless.

Before that moment, Colleen had never let herself believe that it was okay for her to do what she wanted—to spend money on her passion.

In that moment, Colleen realized it was not selfish to

spend money on herself. She saw that it was actually a contribution to the family. When she was involved with her dogs or in talking about them, she became so lit up with enthusiasm that it became contagious. Her husband and daughter loved being around that kind of energy. The family was better off when she was taking care of herself. By following her passion, she was an inspiration to others.

Maybe what you really want to do is raise orchids, but you don't do so because the expenses seem too much. Maybe it's model railroads. But you don't do it because you think your spouse won't approve. Of course you haven't talked about it; you just assume that you can't. It might be climbing mountains, taking accordion lessons, a weekly trip to the spa, a weekend retreat, new clothes, a concert, or a sumptuous night out.

What would you love to do? What would you give yourself if you were your best friend? What would you do that at first glance might seem selfish—but if you did it, you might feel more alive, more fulfilled, and more pleasant to be around?

I have a client who started out with one dance class, one night a week. Now he is taking salsa, tango, and swing dancing. He can't get enough. The people in his life love the enthusiasm this has created in him. He tells me he has more energy, and he is more positive and sure of himself. He has more to give others, because he is doing something for himself.

Now that you can see through this myth that it is self-ish to take care of you, what is it that you could do for yourself? What can you do to take the first step? Take it.

This point is not an excuse to ignore the needs of others in your life or to be irresponsible, nor is it promoting "retail therapy"—the buying spree to try to overcome unhappiness or loneliness. Blindly consuming only for yourself is not the answer.

You should, however, spend money on things or experiences that truly restore you, that energize you and give you the opportunity to be more helpful to others. Go ahead, do something truly special for yourself. The only person's permission you need is your own.

I Can't Charge
What I'm Worth

Not everyone reading this book is self-employed, but this chapter is specifically for those who are. Many of my self-employed clients charge less than what they are worth. Many people do not charge market rate for the services they provide, or even close to it.

Mary is a client of mine who works for a large business-consulting firm. For her services, the firm charges $350 an hour. No one even flinches at this rate, because it is the going rate.

Another client, David, is the sole proprietor of his own business-consulting practice. He does work comparable to Mary's, but he charges $85 an hour. Granted, there is a distinction between a large consulting firm and a sole proprietor. You would expect the large firm to charge more, as they have access to more resources and have to cover a higher overhead. But $265 more an hour?

David does quality work, but he works too long and too hard. I have encouraged him to raise his rates. I told him it would not be at all unreasonable to charge $150 an hour, and if he did, he could cut down the amount of time he spends at work by a third or more, and still earn the same amount of money.

Rarely can self-employed people offer me any information about what rates the market is charging. I get, "That's what my clients are willing to pay me." Or, "I can't charge more than that!" Their comments are based on their own subjective opinions, which are often wrong.

I tell people, "You should charge as much as you can get out of your mouth and not choke."

If you are charging $65 an hour and you know your competitors are charging $125 an hour, you have undervalued yourself. Is it because you are only half as capable as the other person? Not likely. Even if you have a hard time getting yourself to bill at that higher rate, you could easily charge $95 an hour. That would be almost a 50% increase in your billable rate, and that adds up to a lot of money on an annual basis. It might make the difference between just getting by and being able to afford some of the goals you are passionate about.

Here is the process I use with my undervalued self-employed clients. We first do a little research on what the market is charging for comparable work. Then we go through an exercise that asks the person to determine the value of his or her own work, based on the going rate and market conditions. We discuss what they really need and what they feel they deserve to make. Based on our research, we arrive at an amount that the person is comfortable with. If it's $125 an hour, I tell them, "Okay, in the next week, I want you to say out loud 100 times, 'I charge $125 an hour.'"

You can say it to the mirror, in the car to yourself, to your husband, or to your dog. But you have to get it out of your mouth 100 times: *I charge $125 an hour.*

For the first three attempts, most people often can't even say the words without stumbling. They offer up a tentative half-sentence that they are not really committed to. After about thirty times, it gets easier. By seventy-five times, it begins to feel like a favorite pair of slippers. By the hundredth time, the person is ready to say to their next client, "I charge $125 an hour."

A business counselor offered another helpful point. Once you have stated your rate to a client, you need to stop talking. You need to get a response before you say another word. Self-employed people often feel insecure when talking about their rates, so they try to make the other person feel comfortable. They state their rate, and then without allowing the customer to respond, quickly gloss over it by saying, "Oh, I charge $65 an hour, but it varies. It depends on the job. It depends what you have in your budget. I'm willing to negotiate. I work in different ways. . . ."

Tell the client your rate, and then stop talking. The client will let you know if he or she thinks the amount is too high. He or she might ask you how you developed it, or allude to another business that charges less. If so, tell that person why you provide more value than that other business. However, more times than not, the client will just accept your rate without discussion.

I know a self-employed art director who, when asked to place a bid on a job, estimates the cost of the project and comes up with a figure. He tells the client, "I ran the numbers on this project, and based on the work you want done, I came to an overall project cost of $10,000, including expenses." Then he shuts up.

He waits for a response. Sometimes, it's an immediate yes. Other times, he is questioned for more details of his estimate. He then shares the exact number of hours he has estimated for research, design, meetings, and materials, and tells the client his hourly rate. "When I put it all together," he says, "it comes up to $10,332. I rounded it down to $10,000 as a package price." Once again, he shuts up.

Again, he gets a response. If the client cannot afford what he is proposing, he or she tells him. If so, he then asks the client, "What did you have in mind, then? What is in your budget?" Based on this response, he can turn down the job, he can decide to lower the scope of the work, he can see if they can raise their budget 10–20%, or he can accept the lower figure. He always knows his own bottom line prior to the meeting.

However, if he does accept the lower amount, he will say, "Tell you what, I'm going to do this job. I like it and I want to work with you. I will make an exception. But now you know what my standard rate is, so on future projects we need to work toward that goal. Will that work for you?" On nearly every occasion, when the next project does come along, the client is prepared to meet his higher asking price.

When you state what you are worth and stand behind it, it then becomes the client's responsibility to accept your rates or not. You are not responsible for that decision. Your responsibility is to do quality work and to charge what you are worth. Your clients are responsible for the other half of the relationship, and if they believe you are too expensive, they will let you know. Then you can choose to proceed with the project or not.

For some clients, your rates *will* be too expensive. These clients may need to go somewhere else, and you might even suggest someone to whom they can go.

If you decide to accept a job below your rates, do so for the right reasons. You might want to cover some downtime, really like the client or the project, or see it as an inroad with a promising client that may bring you a lot of work down the line. You might decide to donate some of your services. My business counselor has what he calls a "tithe" client—one person in his client base who otherwise cannot afford him, but to whom he donates his services.

Recently, the art director did a job for someone at half his going rate. He did so because of the client's passion for what they were trying to accomplish. He wanted to help that person succeed.

If you do quality work, people will almost always be happy to pay you what you are worth. If they aren't, then you don't want them as a client. But in order to earn the rate you are worth, you must learn to get the message out of your mouth.

When I first went into business, I charged a set amount per hour. I knew it was low, but I was building my business from the bottom up. After getting established, I allowed my rates to rise to their market level. But for my clients who came aboard in my early years, I continued to bill them at the lower rate for some time. I figured they had helped me to get started, and it was a way to pay them back.

At long last, I decided to have all my clients pay the same rate. I sent out a letter to my old clients telling them that I had to raise their rates to be in conformity with everyone else. I agonized over the letter. I knew that it was a steep increase for many of them.

I was rewarded with a pleasant surprise. I got back a stack of responses in the mail. Overwhelmingly, they said,

"It's about time. I support your decision completely. Good for you!"

Two clients told me they were unable to afford the increase. One called me and said, quite emotionally, just how much she appreciated my work. She sincerely thanked me for the help I had given her. She told me she just couldn't afford the higher rates.

I decided to work out a deal with her. I could find a way to make room for anyone who would call and thank me in such a sincere way.

There is nothing wrong with charging what you are worth. There is nothing wrong with charging what the market will bear. It is what people expect you to do. Usually, the only obstacle is your recognition of your own true worth.

Find out what the market charges. Visit the business section of your library. Get on the Internet. Call up other businesses that are in your market and ask them for their rates. If someone is charging a lot more or a lot less, find out the difference between his or her service and yours. Talk to associates in your same profession whom you respect. Ask them what they charge.

After you gather the research, sit down and determine what you are going to charge. Make sure it will cover your costs. Remember that if you are self-employed, you don't receive a benefits package. You have to have money to cover your health care, taxes, overhead, and retirement.

Make allowances for your other long-term goals.

Even though we may resist coming to terms with it, we often *do* know how valuable our work is. We need to acknowledge the value of our own unique attributes and skills and charge appropriately.

I met with a woman who was starting her own business as a computer consultant. She had left her company as a programmer to go out on her own and do programming work for small businesses. She had a great deal of trouble coming to terms with what she should charge. It was very difficult for her to charge near what the market was charging for comparable services. We determined that she should be in the neighborhood of $95 an hour.

I asked her to make a list of the services she provided. Then on a second list I had her write down all the reasons that she should charge $95 an hour. What was special about her? Why should anyone choose her over her competitors? Why should a prospective client hire her?

By the time she was done with her lists she was convinced. She told me, "Well, with this kind of a background, knowledge, expertise, and experience, I am worth it!"

After that point she had no trouble getting her hourly rate out of her mouth without choking. She was able to quote her rate confidently, stand behind it, and feel good about it.

Another client of mine recognizes his ability to synthesize ideas and information faster than anyone he knows.

He saves his clients time and expense by assimilating information upon which to make important business decisions. They count on his ability, and he is able to command a higher hourly rate than others might charge. His clients repeatedly hire him back.

Charge what you are worth. No one else is going to raise your rates. Do the necessary research and determine the appropriate amount. Then revisit and, if necessary, update your rates annually. Your costs will undoubtedly go up because of inflation, so your billing rate may need to go up, as well.

Get this idea off to a good start—take a walk around the block and say *out loud* 100 times, what you are really worth.

I Will Be
Satisfied Later

Fred Lomax owns a corporate marketing company in Tucson, Arizona. He travels two or three days a week visiting companies in the Southwest and California, and he earns a six-figure income doing so. His regional approach to business is one of the reasons behind his financial success.

A company in Los Angeles offered Fred a large contract to do some work. While flying to Los Angeles to meet with the firm, Fred had an opportunity to reflect on his successful career—and the hectic and stressful lifestyle that it demanded. He related this story.

"I sat staring out the window of that 737 at 25,000 feet, seeing the surface of the world move slowly past my field of vision. I began to ponder the fact that as every cloud and mountaintop passed by, I was being carried farther from home. As it was, I had hardly seen my kids for the last week, and now this trip would keep me away from them for another three days. And for what? More money?

"I realized that in stepping on that plane, I had made more than a commitment to a business deal and to a career. I had also committed myself to miss out on the opportunity to spend those days, at least part of those days, with my family—and those were days that I would never be able to recover. When the stewardess went by, I felt like asking her to tell the pilot to turn the airplane around."

After relating this story he said, "You know, I'm not ready to quit my work. But I am really questioning what is truly important in my life. My daughter is going to graduate from high school next year—and then she's gone. This is the last year she will be at home. Is this the year I want to be traveling three or four days a week? My son is a thriving fifth grader. Fifth grade boys need their dad around. And my wife? I adore her. I love being with her. And I miss her when I'm gone."

A moment over the mountains in a 737 changed Fred's life. He asked, "Is it really the money that makes me happy? Is that what's most important in my life?" And the answer led him to a decision.

When Fred returned from his business trip, he announced to his family that he was going to shift his marketing focus to serve only companies located in the Tucson and Phoenix area. It would probably result in less money for awhile, but it would allow him to be where he wanted to be—close to them.

We know that money can't buy everything—yet many of us spend most of our precious time and energy in pursuit of it, often at the expense of our health, well-being, and family.

What we all want is happiness. But happiness isn't necessarily earned by working hard or making more money. For many of us, it comes as a result of simply allowing ourselves to be more satisfied with our lives as they are—not someday, but *now.*

When Fred Lomax got that call from a client with a lucrative job offer in Los Angeles, he accepted immediately. He had programmed himself to do so. He rationalized, "That's more money in the bank. We'll be able to do more. We'll be able to buy more. We'll have a higher standard of living. Great. Of course I accept."

He was on automatic pilot. In making this decision, he wasn't accounting for the cost to his family, or for his own deeper personal needs. The monetary reward was there, but was it leading him to more satisfaction with his life, or was it taking him away from what he valued most?

Few people are able to find total satisfaction and contentment in work alone. We also need relationships with others in our lives—and the time needed to invest in those relationships. We often find ourselves too busy to spend time with those we love, and the rewards of our long hours of toil are rarely sufficient to fill the resulting void.

To find harmony and balance in our lives, we may need

to implement changes. That may mean doing what we want, rather than what everyone else expects. Is your career like a high-speed airplane flight, carrying you ever farther from what and who you love? Have you subscribed to the myth that if you work doggedly now, that you will find satisfaction later? That the money you will earn will be the answer to all your problems?

Perhaps it's time to gaze from your high altitude seat and observe the world passing by far below. Are you missing out on anything important? Are you missing any important stops. Or are you actually heading in the direction you want? If so, relax and enjoy the ride. But if you sense some discord in your speed or direction, perhaps it's time to ask what you could do to be more satisfied now.

Is it possible you could be more satisfied now by realizing how prosperous you already are?

Is that next promotion, or that extra money that you are going to earn, or that new client you are going to take on, really going to bring you that much more satisfaction? Or is it going to be taking you away from those things or people that are most important to you?

If just for a moment you would be willing to say, "More money won't bring me happiness," you could look at that new promotion or that new job with all the travel and say, "Hmm, what's really important here?"

A friend said once, "There is one thing a company can never give back to you, and that is the time you give them."

There is a trade-off in any job. You are trading time for money. Is the extra time you'd have to spend if you take that extra promotion really worth the extra money that you'd receive? Will more money really solve your problems? Will it really bring you more happiness?

Life is about choices. We don't have to live on automatic pilot. We can question some of the beliefs that we hold that keep us on the same old path.

I have a client who worked at a large and fast growing company. She had worked there long enough to amass a large portfolio of stock options. These were available to her if she decided to quit. However, if she worked until January, three months away, she would receive another $50,000. If she stuck it out until July, she would get $115,000.

I did a long-term retirement calculation for her. It showed that if she quit in January, she'd run out of money at age ninety-four. If she quit in July, she'd make it to age ninety-seven. She had three choices. She could quit right away, she could quit at the end of January in time to be home for her kids at the end of the school year, or she could quit July 31, and collect the extra $65,000.

She told me, "Well, that extra $65,000 would be nice. I think I'll stick around until August for that." She went home and told her husband and two kids that she was going to stick it out. She told them it would really make a difference.

She went back to work. Within weeks, she was frustrated and upset. She told me, "I don't want to do this anymore. I'm done. I'm ready to move on. I want to be with my family."

She resolved to quit her job and leave by January 31 and forfeit the extra $65,000. But she didn't tell her family about it for a few days. One night at dinner, she let it slip out that she had decided to quit.

Her kids dropped their forks and said, "What did you say?"

She said, "Well, I'm going to quit at the end of January because I really want us to spend the summer together."

The kids leapt up from the table. They ran around to their mother. They grabbed her around the neck and kissed her. They were ecstatic.

She had no idea how much those six months meant to them. She was heartbroken that they hadn't expressed their disappointment earlier that she was going to work longer, and she was deeply moved that they wanted her home.

Maybe more money is not what we want in life. Maybe it is about those close to us throwing their arms around us and appreciating us for being with them, for sharing our lives with them now.

Maybe we should be investing now in the pursuits and relationships that are dearest to us, rather than putting them off because of concerns over money.

Marsha is a client of mine. She's fifty-seven. She has worked for an airline for nearly 30 years as a flight attendant. She is one of the most vital and dynamic women I have ever known. When she came to see me, we talked about her airline's stock plan and her portfolio. I asked her, "How much longer are you going to work?"

"Well," she said, "The union is renegotiating and if I stick it out until the next contract is signed, my retirement will probably be better."

"What do you want to do after you retire?" I asked. "What are you going to do with all your extra time?"

"Oh, no problem!" She jumped out of her chair completely animated. "I am going to be an actor!"

"You are?"

"Yeah, I'm taking acting classes. I'm learning how to put on make-up and how to analyze a script and take on a role. I have a diction coach, and I am learning how to project my voice and to utilize my whole body in the acting process."

"Marsha that's great!" I said.

"I have an agent now. Maybe I can do some modeling too. I think I might do okay with it."

In addition to her talent, Marsha is a very striking woman with gorgeous gray hair. She looks beautiful for her age. She has found herself as an actress in high demand.

I have seen her from time to time over the past three

years. The last time she came in, she told me that she was getting so many calls to audition for commercials that she had decided she didn't have time to do her airline job any more. She now does acting and modeling exclusively.

She could have stayed at her old job, but for thirty years she had rehearsed the same line, "You want decaf or regular?" and she couldn't say it any more. She found a way to be more satisfied now by making some movement toward a passionate area in her life.

Are there things you can do to be more satisfied now? Step back from your life and reflect on it a bit. Ask yourself where it is taking you and why. Challenge some of the underlying belief systems that have propelled your life to where it is.

How can you be more satisfied in your life *now*? More money is not the answer. But if you allow yourself to be more satisfied by what you already have and use what you have more consciously, you will find more happiness than money can ever buy.

PART II

How to Create Your Own Personal Spending Plan

INTRODUCTION

By now, I hope you have gained some new and refreshing perspectives on your relationship with money. We have questioned many of the prevailing myths involving money—myths that have created an automatic belief system about money and a set of automatic responses to it. Perhaps this inquiry has brought to light some of your behaviors that were sustained by these false beliefs or misunderstandings.

Hopefully, you can begin to question some of these beliefs and make responses to money more consciously. You now see that you have choices, you do not have to respond as you have in the past. You have permission to break the rules, to think about money in a way that is different than the norm.

The second part of the book is for those who want to take this process a step further. It is one thing to philosophically understand the need for change, and it is quite another to follow a plan that guides your financial life. In order to manifest such productive change, you need to develop a structure and implement it.

Each of us has goals we want to accomplish. In the second part of the book, I will provide a format and structure for accomplishing some of the things you would like to happen in your life—things that, perhaps, you didn't think were possible to achieve.

I will present this plan in three parts. The first will show you how to gather facts about your personal spending habits and obligations. The second will show you how to identify and determine your goals. The third puts it all together into a Personal Spending Plan enabling you to accomplish your most important goals *without* deprivation.

CHAPTER 22

Budgets Don't Work—Just the Facts, Please

The only way people are able to make effective and lasting change in their financial life is by first gaining a clear understanding of their starting point—in other words, where their finances currently stand. The way to do that is to start with the facts.

Once you first get clear about where you spend money—and then determine what is really important in your life—you will be able to find the money to accomplish what you want.

Most of us do not take the first step, taking the time to understand how much money we spend and what we spend it on. In fact, we often are afraid to see where our money really goes. We fear that there is not enough to make ends meet, and so we are hesitant to look.

I have seen many of my clients experience a dramatic and positive shift in their financial situation simply by going through the structured process of understanding how their money is currently being spent, and then incorporating their goals into a viable plan—a Personal Spending Plan.

You might discover, much to your surprise, that you already have enough money in your life to accomplish many of your goals *and* live a satisfied life.

Many people have tried their hand at budgeting and have found one thing: *Budgets don't work.* Budgets don't work for the same reason that diets don't work. They address the wrong problem. Diets focus on deprivation, and for most people, budgets do, too.

There is another reason budgets don't work. Most people simply don't write everything down. They write down the expenses they know off the top of their head: their mortgage or rent, their car payment, insurance, and utilities—the well-known recurring bills. Maybe they put in food, but they leave off everything that is more discretionary—their pet bills, haircuts, books, and magazines. They don't include parking and coffee breaks and eating out.

Typically, a person will say, "Well, I make $4,000 per month and my budget says I spend $2,500. So how come I never get ahead? How come I always end the month with more debt on my credit card?"

Thus begins the recurring monthly mystery: Where does it all go? It doesn't make sense. The reason it doesn't make sense is that most people don't base how much they spend on facts. It's amazing, however, the change in behavior that occurs automatically when people see the facts before them.

Mike and Roslyn Williams came to see me because they were spending more than they were making. When I asked them where they spent their money, they were unable to tell me. Their home situation was typical—Roslyn stayed home with the kids, planned the meals, and took care of most household matters. Mike worked long hours as the family breadwinner.

We went through the exercise of reviewing and writing down everything they spent on a monthly basis. It became clear during this exercise that there were certain things Mike had been nagging Roslyn about for years that had never changed. When we came to the line item for groceries, I could see him rubbing his palms together in expectation. He couldn't wait to get into this one.

Before we could get very far, he blurted out, "She spends way too much on groceries. I have been telling her that for years."

"Well, you don't understand," she retorted. "You just don't know what it takes to feed everybody. You just don't know what it costs!"

Mike turned to me. "Ask her how often she goes to the

grocery store!"

I looked at Roslyn questioningly.

"Oh, I go every day," she responded, as though it were what everyone did.

"Ask her where she goes," Mike continued.

I played along, once more looking at Roslyn over the top of my glasses.

"Well. . . the corner convenience store," she said.

"You go to the corner convenience store everyday to buy your family's groceries?" I asked.

"Oh, yeah," she said. "It's right down the block. It's so handy."

"Okay," I asked her, "How much do you spend on groceries?"

She said, "Oh, I don't know. It's expensive for a family of four."

We had to go through her checkbook for the last three months and add up the money spent on groceries. It came to $750 per month. For a husband, wife, a three-year-old and a five-year-old, it seemed like a lot of money.

Roslyn stared at the number before her on the desk. Then she looked me in the eye and said, "Okay, that's it."

Roslyn committed to meal planning and to go to the grocery store no more than twice a week. "And no more buying groceries at the corner store," she said.

No one had to say a word to bring about this transformation. Her husband had been nagging her for fourteen years, and it had not done a thing to alter the situation. He had been trying to tell her what to do and how to run the household, but he had not helped her to see the facts clearly. His approach had been based on the premise that she was wrong, and her reaction had always been, "Well, thank you very much, but until you stay home and take care of the children, and make all the meals—get out of my domain. It is none of your business."

In my office, she changed her attitude on the spot, and it happened for one reason only: she took the facts into account. When she saw how much money she was really spending, she made the decision to change her behavior.

The beauty of financial planning is that the facts will always show you what direction to take. When Roslyn saw the $750 on a piece of paper in front of her—that was it. She decided to spend less money on groceries.

Three months later, Mike and Roslyn came back in for a review. Roslyn had reduced the family's grocery bill to $450 a month!

Like Roslyn, you might *think* you are spending $150 a month on something when you are actually spending $300. Clients will swear that they spend a certain amount on something, but when they gather the facts, they are usually spending more. Until you gather the facts, you will be delusional about how much money you are actually spending on what.

The first step in developing a Personal Spending Plan is

to get very clear about the facts—finding out exactly where *all* your money is going.

List all your monthly expenses on the Monthly Expenses sheet (found in the Appendix)—not what you *think* they are, but what they actually are. Some parts of this process are easy. There are things like house payments and car payments that rarely change, and there are things like groceries or utilities that tend to go up or down, depending on the time of year. For these variable items, I suggest you do a three- or a five-month average.

Go through your checkbook and write down every penny that you spend over a three- to five-month period; then do the same with your credit card bills.

For cash expenses, like eating in restaurants, parking, dry cleaning, and your morning latte, you may need to make an estimate—but be as realistic as possible.

I love to ask clients how much they last got out of the ATM and what they spent it on. Rarely, if ever, can they say where the money went.

Keep track of what you spend cash on for a week or two, then extrapolate this spending to give you a monthly amount. Morning coffee is $1.50 a day, parking is $7. Lunch out is $6, the afternoon snack is $3, dry cleaning is $10 a week. Dinner out two nights a week, that's $35. Entertainment is $25 a week. Add all this up. It works out to over $700 a month! And we wonder where our money goes.

Even if you don't want to keep track of your cash expenses for a week's time, at least sit down for five minutes and estimate what you need on a daily basis for cash items. Include this amount in your Monthly Expenses sheet.

Ideally, it would be great if you kept track of your cash expenses on an ongoing basis. But if that is too much for you, at least get it accurate once. This way, you have a place to start, and you can include that figure in your Monthly Expenses sheet.

You could even use this information to add a little bit of discipline to your life. Once you get a figure for cash items for the week, go to the ATM or the bank at the start of each week and give yourself that much money—but that's all you get for these items for the week. You have to make it last. That's what you get for movies or eating out, or whatever you spend cash on. No more asking for additional cash back on your debit card during the week—just to have cash in your pocket or to make up for buying that thing you just couldn't pass up.

A question I like to ask clients is what amount do you believe you spend on dining out per month? Invariably, they underestimate this figure. At seminars, I ask people to tell me off the top of their heads how much they spend in restaurants. People might say that they spend $150 a month, but when they go back over the actual expenses from their credit cards and checkbooks, they usually find that their restaurant bills are much higher.

No more than three times in eight years of seminars has somebody nailed right on the nose how much he or she actually spends in restaurants. Estimate this figure realistically by answering the following: How many breakfasts do you buy in a week, including weekends? What is the average amount you spend? Do the same for lunches and for dinners. Be sure and include drinks, dessert, and tips. Multiply the weekly figure by four to get the monthly amount you are spending.

If you are like most people, it will probably be higher than you thought. But at least you'll know it's accurate, because it is based on the facts.

Another favorite line item on the Monthly Expenses sheet is for hobbies.

Once at a seminar, one of the wives in the audience asked me to question her husband about how much he spends on his fishing hobby.

I almost had to pry it out of him, because he was sure that whatever number he came up with, it would be taken away from him in next month's spending plan.

Finally, he said "Oh, about $35 a month." His wife laughed. "Well maybe $50," he added. She laughed again. He really didn't know. I told him to go back for the last five months and get a "fishing hobby" figure to put into their Monthly Expenses sheet. Only by knowing how much he actually spends can they begin to know for sure where their money goes.

You need to write down everything that you spend money for. I know this sounds like a daunting task, but your Monthly Expenses sheet needs to include everything—mortgage payments and real estate taxes, retirement and college funding, insurance on your home and family, health insurance and doctor's bills, transportation (including parking, licenses, and repairs), the amount you repay each month on credit cards, utilities and repairs, groceries, dining out, clothing, entertainment, recreation, gifts, gardening expenses, vacations, children's allowances, school expenses, taxes, contributions, dry cleaners, haircuts, postage, newspapers, baby-sitters, counseling and massage sessions, pets, diaper service, music. . . all the expenses that consume your hard earned money. Just write them down and don't decide yet whether you can afford them or not.

If, once you have them written down, they add up to more than you make, *don't change the numbers!* That is the natural response. "This shows I am spending $3,500 a month and I am only bringing home $3,000. So I'll only spend $200 on meals out, not $350. I'll only spend $275 on groceries not $425. . . ."

Don't touch those numbers! Don't try to force them to balance. We need to complete an exercise in goal-setting first. Afterwards, we will have a chance to revisit the fact sheet.

People often resist this exercise because they think that if they add all this stuff up they won't be able to do those activities they enjoy anymore. They assume they do not have enough money. The obvious response is not to keep track, but to make more money. They equate keeping track with budgets, and budgets are about deprivation.

Wrong Answer.

A Personal Spending Plan is not based on deprivation.

In a Personal Spending Plan, determining what you spend your money on is only the first step. It establishes a foundation for your Personal Spending Plan based on facts, so that you can then go on to step two.

Step two is to incorporate your life and financial goals—your dreams and passions—into your plan. So let's do it.

CHAPTER 23

Goal Setting—
Passions Included

Another reason budgets don't work is that they don't incorporate funding of goals. A budget is a restrictive device that creates deprivation. It doesn't make allowances for dreams. Budgets fail because they are not a realistic guide to our true and complete money needs.

A Personal Spending Plan is predicated on including goals in your financial planning.

In determining goals, the first thing to do is to brainstorm—write down all the goals you can imagine. Everyone is really good about writing down the "have to" goals: retirement, college, paying off credit card debt. These fly onto the paper immediately. Go beyond these traditional goals—all the normal "shoulds." Ask "What would I do that would really enrich my life? What is it that I am really passionate about?"

Abbey Kappler has a great interest in the work of

Christo, the artist who creates huge works of art, such as wrapping Biscayne Bay in pink plastic, and planting thousands of open umbrellas in California and Japan. He used 170 workers and 90 rock climbers to drape the Reichstag, a well-known landmark in Berlin, with a million square feet of silver fabric, and then he tied it off with 10 miles of blue cord.

One of Abbey's goals was to be able to afford to go to a Christo exhibit every two or three years. We included this in her financial goals.

I have another client couple whose passion is landscaping. Their yard is a masterpiece, a regular botanical garden—cover of *Home and Garden* stuff. Every season, they plan and shape and sculpture their grounds in a beautiful and inviting way. They are very passionate about it. This is where their extra money goes, and we have provided a line item for it in their Personal Spending Plan.

I have a client whose Personal Spending Plan includes a line item for bike riding. He stays up with the latest in bike technology and racing, and spends a fair amount of money on specialized bike parts and bike expeditions. Another client has a line item for going to live music concerts every year. Another woman takes chemotherapy patients out for meals, or buys them things they need. She has a line item for this in her Personal Spending Plan. A man who has a passion for bagpiping allocates money to include the cost of the bagpipe and the lessons in his financial planning. He even invested in a small bagpipe he can take on backpacking trips—blowing his bagpipes in the wilderness at dawn!

So you see, financial planning and goal-setting can be fun if approached properly. I want you to recruit the services of your imagination and dream. I do not want you to consider obstacles.

Take the next ten minutes to write down all your goals on the Goal Brainstorming Sheet found in the Appendix. Include the obvious ones that pop into your mind right away, the ones you feel you have to fund. But then let the playful part of your mind take control. Get outside your normal thinking and dream a bit. Write down those things that would bring you immense joy.

Some people have difficulty with this goal-setting exercise. There is a deep belief of "Oh, I can't spend money on *that*. That's frivolous, that's just a dream. I can't do it." But write down your dreams even if you don't think they are possible.

Whenever I hear people tell me they can't do something, I think of Jolene Winslow.

Jolene is a woman who emigrated here from South Africa. She is an administrative employee for a county government agency, and she doesn't make much money. When it came time to list her goals, she only wanted one thing: To be able to return to South Africa every three years to see her family. But she said, "It's just not possible with what I make. I'll never be able to do it."

We included this goal and followed through to completion her Personal Spending Plan. Ultimately, it showed that, despite her meager salary, she could in reality afford to go home—and all she had to do was to save $47 each month. She burst into tears when she saw that she was actually going to be able to see her family every three years.

Write down those goals. Don't allow the perceived obstacles to short-circuit the process. Don't let your automatic belief that you can't do something get in the way.

Many people have never established an ambitious dream and then followed through with a viable financial plan to accomplish it. However, you *can* do it.

The next step is to prioritize your goals. Given limited resources, determine which goals you will allocate resources to first. On the Goal Timeframe Sheet (in the Appendix) decide on your definition for *Immediate, Short-term,* and *Long-Range*. These categories do not refer to the time when you will accomplish them, but rather to the time when you will begin to fund them.

For instance, retirement is a long-range goal, but you may want to be funding it now. So it goes in the "immediate" category. Making a documentary film may be a goal of yours, but you may not want to allocate resources to it for a few years yet. Put this in the "long-range" category.

There is no fixed time frame for what each of these categories means. You need to determine the distinctions between immediate, short-term, and long-range. Remember, the distinction is not when you want to accomplish the goal, but when you want to begin funding it. Now, divide your goals into three categories: *Immediate, Short-Term* and *Long-Range*, assigning an "I," "ST," or "LR" for each.

Next, choose your top three items from each category and place them on your Prioritized Financial Goals Sheet in the Appendix. These are your financial goals—the things that, taken together, represent what you "should" fund, as well as the things you really love and want to fund. These represent the top nine goals upon which you will focus your resources.

If you are a couple, each of you come up with your own list, while your partner does the same. Then put them together and agree upon the top nine.

Now it's time for step three: figuring out the cost. For many people, this area is one in which obstacles often arise. They don't want to look at the cost of their dreams because they are afraid they can't afford them.

That was Abbey Kappler's response. How could she possibly go to a Christo exhibit when the events were always in some country far away?

"How much do you think it would cost you?" I asked.

"A lot." She responded.

"Well, you're never going to save 'a lot' of money," I said. "Let's figure out how much it will really cost. Although we don't know which country you'll be traveling to, a good estimate for international airfare is $1,000.

When you are there, how long do you like to stay?"

"Well, I'd really like to stay. . . a week," Abbey responded.

"Okay, let's put in a figure for six nights at a hotel and food for seven days."

We came up with a specific amount for breakfast, lunch, and dinner. We added in some miscellaneous money for gifts or side trips she might be interested in, as well as a small contingency fund.

Once we went through that exercise, we discovered it would cost her $3,000 to go to an exhibit every three years. We divided the $3,000 into 36 months, and the result was that she would have to save $83.33 a month in order to accomplish her goal.

"Well, I can do that!" she exclaimed.

She set up a savings account and began to deposit $85 a month toward her trips.

Eighty-five dollars a month was an amount she could grasp, and it certainly was a lot more achievable than "a lot of money." Passions and dreams do not have to be denied because they seem expensive. Once you know exactly what they will cost and commit to working toward them, they are often achievable.

Another client, Maureen, has a simple passion—her friends—so she includes an amount in her Personal Spending Plan called "community." It provides for two weekends away with friends per year, one social dinner a week, and enough money to do six random acts of kindness. This is her number-one financial goal, and she sets aside $163 a month for this category.

Dining out is one of the joys of my life. When I was growing up, we could rarely afford to do so. When we did, it was a big thrill, and it still is—with my family, going to a restaurant is a special event. My daughter Marie always puts on a fancy dress, and it's a great occasion. If I walk out in my jeans, she says, "Mom. . . We're going out to dinner. You need to dress up!" So going out to dinner once a week is in my Personal Spending Plan. It doesn't cost very much money to bring my family the pleasure and happiness that our special dinners create.

Once you have determined the cost of a goal, divide this by the number of months left until you want to accomplish it. Come up with the monthly amount necessary to save. Don't try and figure out if it is possible yet; just do the work. It might be $25 a month to provide a family in India with a new home twelve months from now. It might be $75 a month to help fund part of your child's college education. It might cost $167 a month for a down payment for a new house in the country ten years from now.

By now, you should have your top nine goals: three immediate, three short-term, and three long-range. Beside each goal should be the total cost, when you want to accomplish it, and a monthly amount necessary.

Now, let's put it all together.

CHAPTER 24

Putting It All Together

The third part of a Personal Spending Plan is to make the all-important lifestyle and spending decisions based on the facts you have gathered. We want to determine how you can alter the way you spend money so that you can indeed accomplish these goals—without deprivation.

The reason you determine your goals prior to making any changes in your spending habits is that without this data, your efforts are doomed to fail. I've never seen people stop spending money simply because they thought they should, or because someone told them to do so. It takes dedication to a deeply held desire to achieve lasting change in your spending habits, and this focus requires a clear definition of what's important to you—your goals.

One of my favorite examples of this kind of dedication is Jeff Saville.

I was leading a seminar for a group of hair salon stylists.

One thing about hair stylists is that a lot of cash goes through their hands in the form of tips. For most of them, it's easy come, easy go. They usually don't know how much they get in tips, and they don't keep track of where they spend it.

I took them through the entire Personal Spending Plan process. I had them do a fact sheet on their current spending, identify their deeper passions and goals, and reassess how they were spending their money in light of those goals.

Three months later, we had a follow-up session.

Before I could start, a young guy in the front row was waving his hand for me to call on him. It was Jeff Saville.

"Um, is there something you would like to share with the group?" I asked.

"Yes," he said. "From the goal-setting exercise you had us do, I got real clear about what my goals were. And I committed to them. I established two goals. I wanted to go to Hawaii or someplace else where it's sunny once every year. . . ."

"That's not a bad goal for someone living in Seattle," I interjected.

He laughed. "Actually, for me it's a necessity," he said, "and I wanted a red Mazda Miata convertible. Those were my goals."

"Sounds reasonable," I said.

"I added up how much I spent on lattés and eating out

in restaurants. In the three months since we were last here, my Hawaii trip is paid for. . . and you passed my red Mazda Miata when you walked in."

I wasn't the only person in the room who was visibly shocked. "How could this be?" I asked. "How could you do that in three months?"

"For three months, I went cold turkey on lattés and I learned to make my lunch and take it to work. I didn't go out for snacks whenever I felt like it, and I ate dinners at home—or let other people take me out and pick up the tab!"

People in the room chuckled.

"Listen, I counted up how many lattés I consumed during the day. Six! Six lattés with tips is $12 a day. I spend an average of $5 a day on snacks. I go out to lunch everyday and spend about $8 every time. So far, that's $25 a day. I work six days a week. That adds up to $600 a month. Cutting a few dinners eating out, I ended up saving nearly $2,000 over a three-month period. My Hawaii trip will cost me $1,100, and the remaining $900 was enough for the down payment on the car. I can now afford the monthly payments from the amount I won't be spending on lattés and lunch everyday."

People in the seminar applauded.

"I'd say you are a pretty committed fellow," I said. "Congratulations."

"Yeah, but here's the thing," he said. "If you had asked

me at the last session how many lattés I drank a day, I would have said six. And if you had told me that I was wasting a lot of money, that I was spending too much—and that all that coffee was bad for me, I would have told you that you had no idea how much energy it takes to cut people's hair everyday. It's not only the haircutting and being on your feet, but also having to keep up the conversation. I would have told you that I couldn't have gotten through my job, talking to those people all day long, if I didn't have my lattés. I would have told you not to tell me how many lattés I can drink during the day. And I would have told you that I don't have the time to make my lunch everyday. I barely make it to work on time, work long hours, and go home dead at the end of the day. That's what I would have said to you.

"Instead, when I saw for myself that the lattés and lunches were costing me $600 a month, I realized I can more than adequately make a car payment and have plenty left over to go someplace sunny and warm every year. I instantly stopped drinking lattés. I got through the caffeine withdrawal—it wasn't a big deal. And I'm getting up early each day to make my lunch.

"It's like, once I realized that I could actually have these things, nothing could stop me!"

Jeff Saville exemplifies a great truism about financial planning. When you clearly determine what you are committed to, and when you clearly understand the facts, you are likely to change your behavior.

With a Personal Spending Plan, you know what is really important to you, and you gain the motivation to alter, sometimes dramatically, how you spend money. This plan is not about deprivation—quite the opposite. In Jeff Saville's case, the result was abundance—attainment of the things he wanted most, and in a very short period of time.

If I had told Jeff Saville not to spend money, he would have felt as if I was trying to deprive him. It would have generated resistance: "Don't preach to me about spending. You can't possibly know what it's like to be in my shoes. . . ." But when he clearly understood that he could go to Hawaii and have his new dream car, simply by changing his spending habits, he altered his behavior immediately. He became self-motivated.

Just like dieting, financial deprivation doesn't work. However, setting your sight on a positive goal aligns your energy toward achieving it. The negative activity just falls away.

That is the reason a Personal Spending Plan works. You first gain an understanding of where your money is going, and then you figure out what it is that you really want. With these two pieces of information, you can easily determine the areas where adjustments in your spending are possible and realistic. In no time at all, your goals become reality—without feeling deprived!

Abbey Kappler now travels to a Christo exhibit every

three years, Jolene Winslow travels home to see her family in South Africa on a regular basis, and Maureen's friends experience six random acts of kindness from her a year.

Each of them first became clear about their spending habits; then they became clear about their goals. Finally, they went back to their fact sheet to determine the areas where changes in spending habits could be made.

The final area where I can help you in your Personal Spending Plan is the determination of where to make the changes—where to reduce?

When you go back to your Monthly Expense Sheet to review expenses, classify them into three categories: *Committed, Somewhat Discretionary,* and *Very Discretionary.*

Committed items are things on which you are obligated to spend money—house payment or rent, utilities, car payment, car insurance. These expenses are not likely to go away, no matter what your goals are.

The *Somewhat Discretionary* category includes things on which you must spend money, but which allow you some discretion on the amount. You have to buy food, for instance, but perhaps you could do so more economically.

The third category are the *Very Discretionary* items, like gifts, eating out in restaurants, clothing, hobbies, snacks, and entertainment. These are the things on which you could really spend a lot less if you chose to, and you want to look here first for money to be reapplied toward your goals.

In this part of the process, you want to reduce the amount you spend on the Very Discretionary and Somewhat Discretionary expenses. First, reduce the amounts so you are at least not spending more than you make. Then, continue to cut back until you free up money to accomplish your goals in the time frame you desire.

Don't be discouraged if you can't fund all your goals the first time you try this process. This round is only the beginning, and as you accomplish a goal, that money can be reallocated to the next goal.

Before you reallocate anything, ask yourself, "How much satisfaction does this bring me?" If you have an item for which you spend money that is very discretionary, but truly brings you a lot of satisfaction, then don't cut that one first. For me, dining out once a week with my family gives me a great deal of satisfaction. If I were to cut that from my spending plan, it would constitute deprivation.

However, I use a great deal of self-restraint when spending money on movies or other forms of entertainment. I don't buy lattés, and I rarely go out for lunch. I pass up a lot of indulgences to save the money necessary to dine out once a week with my family. Though discretionary, some items on your list may need to be put in the "do not touch" category.

When you decide to cut back in a particular area, try not to be overly aggressive at first. The objective is not to deprive yourself, but to gradually steer spending momentum away from things that are of lower value in your life, and toward your true goals. Put the money where it counts the most, and remember that a little saved in a few areas adds up to a lot each month.

One helpful way to keep your goals in front of you is to put your list of goals on your refrigerator or next to your bathroom mirror. When something on which you want to spend money comes up, take a look at your list. Ask yourself, "Is this new leather jacket more important than saving to go to Europe?" By keeping focused on your goals, passing up that leather jacket will not seem like deprivation.

It's all about personal choices based on facts—not sacrifice. It's about funding your goals and living a life right now that is consistent with what is important to you.

The last step is to complete the Personal Spending Plan Worksheet found in the Appendix. In Column A, record what income you receive between the 1st and the 15th, as well as the expenses that are due during that time. Then In Column B, record the income you receive between the 16th and the 31st, along with the expenses for that time period. If you have more bills in one column than income, set aside some income from the other column to pay those bills. By the time you have completed this sheet, you will know what bills will be paid and what goals will be funded from each paycheck.

When compared with the amount of knowledge most people have of their personal finances, just finding out where your money goes in a month is a major accomplishment. To follow through by identifying and writing down your goals is even more rare. To complete the process by reallocating your spending to accomplish your goals—well, happy are the few who dare to venture this far.

Try it. The journey will be worth it.

CHAPTER 25

Where to Go from Here

We hold three misconceptions about money that are almost universal.

The first misconception is: *If I had more money, I would be happier.* I could move to a bigger house. I could get that new car. My investment portfolio could get to the level it needs to be. I could finally get ahead and not struggle so much. I would have more peace of mind. I would have more free time. I could do what I really want to do—happy at last.

The reality is that more money will not give you peace of mind. No doubt you make a lot more than you did on your first job. Is your life more fulfilled because of your additional income? Do you feel freer, more content, more secure, and more alive? Do you have fewer problems now? Do you at last have money figured out? Does more money really bring you happiness? You hope that it does.

The second misconception is: *People who make more than*

I do don't have money problems. We assume that we are alone in not understanding money. When we see another person who earns more money than us, we automatically assume that they must have money figured out.

Just because people make more money than you doesn't mean they are free of the problems with which you wrestle on a daily basis. Most people spend up to the level of their income, and their problems follow right along with them.

Assuming that your basic needs are well-covered, it makes little difference how much money you make—*unless you have a plan.*

We are often "insane" about money—we keep doing the same thing over and over again and expecting a different result. Until you have a plan, life is not going to change. It has little to do with how much you make. It has everything to do with your goals and whether your spending is consistent with those goals. Think about it. What is your life all about? Are you heading in the direction of your true purpose? Is your financial plan leading you toward, or away from that purpose?

The last great misconception about money is: *Someday, one day, it is all going to turn out okay.* When people lay this one on me, I ask them, "Just what is going to happen to make it all turn out? Your next raise? An inheritance? Or maybe winning the lottery?"

I need to tell you this, my friends: *Someday it's not going to turn out—unless you do your part.* You're probably not going to marry the prince or the princess who will bestow instant wealth upon you. You're unlikely to win the lottery. Your next raise won't fix all your problems. It's not going to just work out unless you have a plan that includes your goals and you *implement* that plan.

What would your life be like if you decided to be more satisfied now? What would it be like to have a conscious understanding of money and its role in your life? How would you feel about money if its sole purpose was to provide an avenue to your goals and deeper passions?

We need to better understand the real purpose and potential of money, and how we use or misuse it. Money is simply a medium of exchange. By clarifying our goals, we can put money to work for us instead of the other way around.

The course to success begins by reflecting on why we react and spend as we do, while leaving behind our old beliefs about money. We can then head in a new direction based on knowledge—knowledge founded on *where we are* and *where we want to go.* Getting there then becomes a simple matter of steering and adjustment.

If you wish to change your relationship with money, there are three things you must do.

First, gain a clear understanding of how you spend and what you spend on. Second, incorporate your deeper goals into a financial plan and commit to that plan. And third, allow yourself to be satisfied now.

If you are not satisfied with your life, don't look to money. It will not solve your troubles. Look elsewhere.

But where?

Perhaps the ancient Chinese sage Lao-Tzu is a place to start:

Fame or integrity: which is more important?
Money or happiness: which is more valuable?
Success or failure: which is more destructive?

If you look to others for fulfillment,
You will never be fulfilled.
If your happiness depends on money,
You will never truly be happy with yourself.

Be content with what you have;
Rejoice in the way things are.
When you realize there is nothing lacking,
The whole world belongs to you.

ACKNOWLEDGMENTS

Whenever I read the acknowledgments in a book, I am inspired by the fact that so many people are willing to support others in realizing their dreams. My case is no different.

I'd first like to acknowledge my "Advisory Group," Terry Axelrod, David Goodenough and Ben Reppond. You were with me in the beginning and believed in me in the face of no evidence. Your wise counsel, your support and especially your friendships are very dear to me.

Because of your coaching, Rik Super, this book became a reality. Thank you for having my life be greater than my wildest dreams.

Thanks to my agent, becker & mayer! Thank you Andy Mayer for having the inspiration; Jim Becker for the trip of a lifetime to NY; and to Maggie Stanphill and Alison Herschberg for your support throughout the process.

Thank you Judith Regan, President & Publisher of

ReganBooks. You took a chance on me that will forever change my life. Thanks for being willing.

Thank you Jeremie Ruby-Strauss, my editor at ReganBooks. You're the best jaded editor anyone could ever want.

Thanks to my colleagues, Cicily Maton and Nancy Nelson for their review of the manuscript. Your suggestions were outstanding. And to Kathleen Cotton for thinking of me in the first place.

Thank you is quite inadequate for you, Ward Serrill. Let's say that we both know this book is as good as it is because of your magic. Thanks also to Douglas Serrill for your editing and creative input.

To my staff, Timothy Blair, Anand Skeels, Christopher Minnie, and Shawn Donnelly, it is an honor and a privilege to work with you. Your dedication to serving our clients is truly moving. I want you all on my team forever.

Thank you to my spiritual teachers that throughout my life have shown me the way.

Thank you, Werner Erhard, for assisting me in finding out who I really am and all that's possible in life.

To my family I say thank you for always supporting me. I am so blessed to have you all in my life.

And finally to my clients, thank you for your courage in sharing your lives with me, not just your finances. Thank you for allowing me into your lives in this most intimate way. I consider it a most precious gift.

APPENDIX

To locate fee-only Certified Financial Planners in your area call the National Association of Personal Financial Advisors at 1–888–333–6659 or visit their Web site at http://www.napfa.org.

To request an estimate of your projected Social Security benefits at retirement, call the Social Security Administration at 1–800–772–1213 or visit their Web site at http://www.ssa.gov.

MONTHLY EXPENSES

	Jan.	Feb.	Mar.	Apr.	May	Jun.	Jul.	Aug.	Sept.	Oct.	Nov.	Dec.	TOTAL
Savings & Investments													
Mortgage Payment or Rent													
Interest on Mortgage													
Real Estate Taxes													
Vacation Home Mortgage													
Interest on Mortgage													
Real Estate Taxes													
Transportation													
Auto Loan Payment													
Gas & Oil													
Maintenance & Repair													
Parking													
Licence													
Public Transportation													
Charge Accounts													
Personal Loans													
Household Expenses													
Cable TV													
Children Allowances													
Clothing													
Club Dues													
Eating Out													
Education Expenses													
Electric													
Entertainment													
Family Visits													
Furniture & Decorating													
Garbage													
Gardening													
Gas													
Gifts													
Groceries													
Maintenance & Repair													
Miscellaneous													
Recreation													
Telephone													
Vacation/Camp													
Water													
Taxes													
Federal													
State													

To use this document, photocopy at 141%

MONTHLY EXPENSES

	Jan.	Feb.	Mar.	Apr.	May	Jun.	Jul.	Aug.	Sept.	Oct.	Nov.	Dec.	TOTAL
Insurance													
Life													
Health													
Disability													
Home													
Auto													
Other													
Medical Expenses													
Doctor													
Dental													
Optician/Glasses/Contacts													
Prescriptions													
Vitamins													
Contributions													
Religious													
Charitable													
Other Expenses													
Attorney													
Baby Sitter													
Books/Magazines													
Daycare													
Diaper Service													
Dry Cleaners													
Financial Planner													
Haircuts													
Hobbies													
House Cleaning													
Lattes													
Manicures													
Massages													
Music													
Newspaper													
Other													
Pager													
Pets													
Postage													
Seminars													
Storage													
Taxes													
Therapy													
Total By Month													
Net Income													
Surplus (Deficit)													

To use this document, photocopy at 141%

GOAL BRAINSTORMING SHEET

My financial goals are:

_____

_____

_____

_____

_____

_____

_____

_____

_____

_____

_____

_____

_____

_____

_____

_____

_____

_____

_____

_____

_____

_____

GOAL TIMEFRAME SHEET

Before you can prioritize your goals you need to identify if
they are:

Timeframe

I = Immediate = _____

ST = Short-term = _____

LR = Long-range = _____

Now, in the left margin of the Goal Brainstorming Sheet,
put either an "I", "ST", or "LR" in front of each goal.

PRIORITIZED FINANCIAL GOALS

	Total Cost	Target Date to be Complete	Monthy Amount Necessary

Immediate:

1. _____ _____ _____ _____

2. _____ _____ _____ _____

3. _____ _____ _____ _____

Short-term:

1. _____ _____ _____ _____

2. _____ _____ _____ _____

3. _____ _____ _____ _____

Long-range:

1. _____ _____ _____ _____

2. _____ _____ _____ _____

3._____ _____ _____ _____

PERSONAL SPENDING PLAN
DEVELOPED FOR:

_____

Column A: 1st – 15th

Net Income

Source	Amount
_____	$_____
_____	$_____
_____	$_____
Total	$_____

Column B: 16th – 31st

Net Income

Source	Amount
_____	$_____
_____	$_____
_____	$_____
Total	$_____

Goals/ Expenses	Monthly Amount Due	Cumulative Expense Amount

Goals/ Expenses	Monthly Amount Due	Cumulative Expense Amount

ALSO AVAILABLE
FROM THE AUTHOR

If you would like any of the following please contact
Karen through her Web site at
http://www.KarenRamsey.com or
e-mail her at Ramsey@karenramsey.com.

- Invite Karen to speak at your next conference
- Subscription to Karen's no-load mutual fund model
  portfolio recommendations
- Or if you'd just like to share your insights from
  reading this book

INDEX